RETIREMENT
the PSYCHOLOGY
of REINVENTION

KENNETH S. SHULTZ, PhD

WITH MEGAN KAYE AND MIKE ANNESLEY

Senior Editor Bob Bridle
Senior Art Editor Karen Constanti
Editorial Assistant Alice Kewellhampton
Jacket Art Editor Harriet Yeomans
Senior Producer, Pre-Production Tony Phipps
Senior Producer Stephanie McConnell
Creative Technical Support Sonia Charbonnier
Managing Editors Dawn Henderson, Stephanie Farrow
Managing Art Editor Christine Keilty
Art Director Maxine Pedliham
Publisher Peggy Vance

Written by Megan Kaye and Mike Annesley
Illustrations Keith Hagan

First published in Great Britain in 2016
by Dorling Kindersley Limited
80 Strand, London WC2R 0RL
A Penguin Random House Company

A CIP catalogue record for this book is
available from the British Library
ISBN 978-0-2412-2954-5

Colour reproduction by Altaimage Ltd
Printed and bound in China

All images © Dorling Kindersley Limited
For further information see: www.dkimages.com

A WORLD OF IDEAS:
SEE ALL THERE IS TO KNOW

www.dk.com

CONSULTANT PSYCHOLOGIST

Kenneth S. Shultz, PhD

Professor of Psychology in the Department of
Psychology at California State University, San
Bernardino (CSUSB), Professor Shultz specializes
in issues relating to aging and the workplace. He
teaches classes in industrial and organizational
psychology – as well as aging workforce issues – at
both undergraduate and graduate level. In addition,
he is the Interim Director for the Center on Aging at
CSUSB, which seeks to understand the concerns and
enhance the wellbeing of older people. He has made
more than 100 professional presentations and published
approximately 50 peer-reviewed articles, 10 book
chapters, and four books in his field of specialization.
Professor Shultz was also recently the recipient of his
university's prestigious Outstanding Professor Award.

ACKNOWLEDGMENTS

Kenneth S. Shultz:
I would like to especially thank my wife and colleague,
Dr Deborah Olson, for her support and encouragement
to contribute to this much needed book.

The publisher would like to thank:
Mike Annesley for his help with developing the
contents and reviewing the text; Vanessa Daubney
for editorial assistance; Laura Buscemi for design
assistance; and Vanessa Bird for the index.

CONTENTS

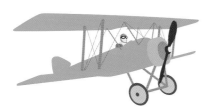

CHAPTER 3
WHEELS IN MOTION
INTO A NEW DAWN

CHAPTER 4
A TIME OF ADJUSTMENT
THE FIRST YEARS OF RETIREMENT

CHAPTER 5
LIVING WELL
LOOKING AFTER YOU AND YOURS

CHAPTER 6
THE NEW YOU
HOW TO REINVENT YOURSELF

FOREWORD

Approximately 25 years ago my father was offered an early retirement package at the age of 55. While physically he was ready to retire from a demanding job at the telephone company, psychologically he was not ready. I was just beginning my research career, and so my interest in the psychological aspects of the retirement process was piqued by my father's experience. Much of the research on retirement at that time (in the early 1990s) was focused on "health and wealth". That is, most economists believed that health and wealth were the driving forces behind the decision to retire. However, a quarter of a century later, and having published several books, book chapters, and numerous articles on the topic of the psychology of retirement since then, I am amazed at the dynamic nature of retirement in the 21st century, as well as the critical importance that psychological factors play in the transition to retirement.

Today retirement can take a number of different forms. This can include volunteer work, starting a second career, taking on the role of caregiver, or more likely, some combination of roles. Retirement has become a very individualized and personal journey for those making the transition from a career to that next phase of life.

Retirement: The Psychology of Reinvention is ideal for anyone who is making the personal journey from full-time work to retirement. Every page is bursting with practical advice that, importantly, is based on a solid underpinning of the most recent and comprehensive scientific research on the psychology of retirement. The text is highly accessible and the scientific findings are translated into visually engaging graphics that everyone can understand.

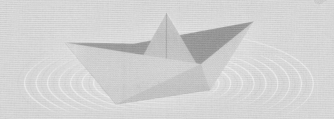

The book covers every stage of the retirement process. Chapter one puts work and retirement in the context of life in the 21st century. Then, chapter two focuses on the importance of early planning for retirement, while chapter three covers the key challenges in the lead-up to the big day. Next, chapter four discusses the transition from work to retirement and the unique challenges faced in the first days, weeks, and months after leaving full-time work. Chapter five covers how best to grow psychologically into the role of retiree and the importance of looking after yourself, as well as those close to you. Finally, chapter six is about the many ways in which you can reinvent yourself in retirement and reach your maximum potential.

Retirement: The Psychology of Reinvention serves as a comprehensive, accessible, research-grounded guide to the psychology of retirement for those increasing number of baby-boomers making the transition from worker to retiree.

Kenneth S. Shultz

Professor Kenneth S. Shultz, PhD

CHAPTER 1

WORK AND LIFE

RETIREMENT IN CONTEXT

SUNSET OR NEW DAWN?

FACING THE FUTURE

We all face retirement in our own way. Some see it as a gift, while others may think of it as a challenge. The key is to approach retirement with optimism, treating it as an opportunity for new kinds of fulfilment.

Retirement, like going to school for the first time or having your first child, is a major life landmark. As such, you're likely to have to come to terms with two major changes: long periods of free time in which to occupy yourself in a satisfactory way; and feelings of loss regarding the structure and purpose that work provides.

How do you feel?

Are you happy and confident about the prospect of retiring, having perhaps found work a burden you're relieved to be free of? Or are you anxious about the change, concerned how you'll cope without the career that occupied so much of your waking time? Sometimes people in the lead-up to retirement describe it as carrying an element of uncertainty: with several options available to them, choosing one way over another seems inherently risky. Excitement is a common response, too: the sense of a new life beckoning, of a long-awaited

THE VIEW FROM HERE

Although we all view retirement in individual ways – depending on our personal circumstances, priorities, and personalities – psychologists have identified three key approaches:

Excessively negative
An unappealing future looms – with a loss of purpose and self-esteem.

Realistically positive
A new phase of positive fulfilment and social engagement is about to begin. You have an array of inner and social resources to draw on.

Unrealistically positive
A new, contented life of leisure and fulfilment will unfold automatically and start immediately.

This is the "happy-ever-after" fallacy, when retirement feels like the solution to all life's problems.

rebalancing, or a freedom from commitment as if a debt had finally been paid off. You're likely to have complicated feelings about retirement, often with a degree of apprehension. This apprehension may be linked to aging, rather than leaving work, and some doubt will centre on the adjustment required to make the best use of a new and very different phase of life.

A golden age?

The quality of your retirement may depend, in part, on your existing circumstances: any unresolved life issues will probably remain difficult, and may be magnified once the distraction of work has gone. It will also depend on your attitude and, in particular, the enthusiasm, energy, and resourcefulness you're able to channel into shaping a new life for yourself. Retirement is a new dawn in the sense that it represents a great opportunity to reinvent or fine-tune your life according to a template of your own making. The best preparation is to reach a level of self-understanding before the big day, and use this as a basis for setting long-term priorities and goals.

WHAT'S IN STORE?

Any or all of the following uncertainties may complicate your attitude to retirement:

AT WORK
How much, if at all, will you miss the following features of work?

- Purpose and self-esteem
- Work community
- Income from employment

IN YOUR NEW LIFE
How well will you adjust to the following new aspects of life?

- More time for yourself
- More time with your partner
- More time at home

OTHER ISSUES
How well will you handle issues in the following aspects of later life?

- Your own health, and that of your partner or family members
- Financial security
- Social or political changes

WILL YOU COPE?

Uncertainty about the future causes people to react in different ways, but psychologists have identified four common responses – which do you identify with?

1 **You dwell on the risks** and dangers, including threats to your emotional security and self-image.

2 **You think you won't cope** when the time comes because, you reason, you've been unable to make a clear plan of action.

3 **You procrastinate**, allowing the uncertainty to continue.

4 **You prioritize safe activities** over challenging or unfamiliar experiences.

There's no single cure-all to these issues, but you could reduce any anxiety linked with uncertainty by, for example, preparing for several different possibilities.

 BRIGHTER LATER

Here are some of the ways in which retirees make good use of their free time and give their life new purpose and structure:

SELF-DEVELOPMENT
- Personal projects
- Some form of work, whether entrepreneurial or supportive
- Volunteer activity
- Learning subjects or skills

FRIENDS AND FAMILY
- New phase of life with partner
- New friendships
- Caring for elderly relatives or grandchildren

LEISURE AND FITNESS
- Holidays, staying with friends
- Use of local leisure facilities
- Walking and other fitness pursuits
- Hobbies

THE SHAPE OF THINGS

HOW WE THINK OF OUR LIVES

When we look back at our past, we see our life experience as having a shape, and not necessarily a tidy one. How does this life view influence the choices we make about retirement?

We all have a sense of the shape of our lives unfolding. Within this trajectory are key developmental phases: babyhood, childhood, the teenage years, and adulthood – which breaks down traditionally into young adult, middle-aged, and senior. Longer life-expectancies are moving back the point at which we think of ourselves as passing from middle-aged to senior. It's often said that you're as old or as young as you feel, and from a psychological perspective this is a valuable idea: it encourages people to realize more of their potential in later life.

A life in the round

When we look at our past, present, and future as a whole, what bearing does it have on our retirement choices?

- If we have a sense of personal progression, we might view

 **LIFE MEMORIES**

One view of retirement is that it's the time for stopping and taking a well-earned rest, after the more energetic activities of earlier life. By the age of, for example, 65 or 70 we've accumulated a store of memories that are emotionally sustaining: they tell us who we are. While it's true that retirement can be a time to relax and enjoy those memories, the happiest people tend to be those who continue to be active – perhaps creating some new memories along the way.

> **Our memory** is our **coherence**, our **reason**, our **feeling**, even our **action**.
>
> **Luis Buñuel**
> Film-maker

retirement as a continuation of that progression, either in a new direction or one related to our previous career.

■ We might think in terms of generations. If we cherish our role within the extended family, travel might become a bigger part of lives – for example, as we visit relatives further afield.

■ If we express our lives in economic terms, we might ask ourselves whether we can continue our current lifestyle in retirement or whether we'll have to scale things back.

The power of other people

Social conditioning plays a large part in our psychological make-up, and at a very basic level this is seen in attitudes to life that are influenced by observing people we regard as our peers. We may aspire to imitate others in the life we perceive they're enjoying. During our working lives our goals with regard to disposable income, lifestyle choices, and material acquisitions may be partly determined in this way. When we look at our lives in the round, we're likely to be conscious of whatever "norms" we can identify around us, even if we've chosen to follow our own path.

Re-writing the script

According to cognitive psychology, everyone has a life script, which they follow consciously or subconsciously. Quite separately from the obvious landmarks of a life, our life script traces the story we habitually use to make sense of our experiences. Sometimes it will generalize in a way that absolves us of blame for our own disappointments: "people always leave me," we might say, and this causes us to act defensively, perhaps keeping romantic involvements at arm's length to pre-empt our being deserted again.

As you approach retirement, it's helpful to take a close look at your life script and identify any ways in which it might throw you off the path to contentment in later life, unless you're able to edit it to reflect the truth of your experience more accurately. The following life statements, for example, are likely to require analysis and revision:

■ I can't function on my own.
■ I don't deserve my good luck.
■ I have no real skills.
■ I'm never myself: I only pretend.

As retirement is above all a time of possibilities, we need to rip up a limiting script and start living more in the moment.

HOW DO YOU MEASURE UP?

Applying a measure to our lives and summarizing our success is appropriate to competitive sport or even perhaps creative achievement – for example, an artist might measure success in terms of the number of exhibitions they've had. Many people today measure their popularity, or that of their website, by the number of internet hits. However, a rich, satisfying life feels good without any need for quantifying confirmation. Indeed, some who assess themselves in this way do so out of insecurity. Here are some aspects of life that can be measured, alongside related aspects that can't:

Measurable	Beyond measure
■ Academic qualifications	■ Lifelong learning
■ Awards and prizes	■ Talents and skills
■ Wealth in financial terms	■ Wealth of experience
■ Cash value of house	■ Emotional value of home
■ Years a relationship has lasted	■ Depth and importance of love
■ Number of friends	■ Quality of friendships

OUR 50s AND 60s

MIDDLE AGE AND AFTER

These are the years of maturity. We've started to be conscious of aging, yet, if we keep ourselves fit and lead a healthy lifestyle, we have a good chance of thriving and satisfying our goals.

Our 50s, in many ways, is a "fulcrum decade", in the phrase coined by sociologist David Karp. For the first time, we're likely to be aware of our aging and start thinking of life in terms of how long we have left. In modern society, where youth remains highly prized, we might start to feel our age in terms of body image and physical capabilities, while remaining young at heart – that is, fluid in attitudes and welcoming of new ideas and technologies.

The happiness U-curve

Research has shown that people in their 50s and 60s tend to be happier than those in their 30s and 40s. The general picture is a U-curve, showing increasing happiness until around 30, dipping in the 30s and 40s, and climbing back up after 46, the global low point. Underlying this rise are several factors relating to the stresses of earlier middle age. For example, those who have achieved career goals may feel contented, while those with children who have left home may feel that a burden has lifted. Another explanation is that people get better at coping, having had plenty of practice by this time.

On the up

After 60, health issues for ourselves or our loved ones may be at the front of our minds. However, as shown by a University of California,

Berkeley study led by Dr Robert Levenson, intelligence and cognitive skills can sharpen, giving us an advantage in employment and in our personal relationships. Above all, the value we find in loving and companionable relationships can exceed all other kinds of happiness.

WHY ARE PEOPLE HAPPIER AT 60?

Happiness has been shown to increase in our 50s and 60s, perhaps because anxieties about career, relationships, and family have settled down. Other explanations include:

- Greater "wisdom", or psychological intelligence, in dealing with life situations.

- Lower aspirations, especially in terms of status, success, and wealth.

- A sense of fulfilment and accomplishment.

- Greater appreciation of life's pleasures.

- Less anxiety about the future, combined with a greater tendency to live in the moment.

- Greater ability to regulate emotions, such as anger, impatience, and jealousy.

- Less concern about satisfying others' expectations.

LOOKING INTO THE DISTANCE

When we find ourselves going to funerals of friends we start to "personalize" death, and the future no longer seems endlessly spacious. This can make us more decisive, unwilling to procrastinate, and eager to start on projects we might have been toying with for years. Retirement gives us the opportunity to get such projects moving, with focus and determination.

THE VIEW FROM 40
Time stretches forward, rich in possibilities. The limitations that prevent our seizing them are to do with our skills, responsibilities, and approach to risk.

THE VIEW FROM 60
We imagine we might have up to two decades to progress our personal development and start and finish anything new. We're impelled to start without delay.

early 50s

THE PRIME OF LIFE?

In a sample of **700 college alumnae** of all ages, it was women in their **early 50s** who most often described their lives as **"first-rate"**. The answers they gave showed that the women in this age group were the ones who were the most **confident, involved, secure, and broad-minded**.

CRYSTALLIZED INTELLIGENCE

Dr Art Kramer, who has studied aging at the Beckman Institute in the US, is one of a group of scientists who have found that, as we enter our 50s, we often have an increased capacity for "crystallized intelligence" – knowledge gained from experience over the years.

Richard E. Nisbett, a cognitive psychologist at the University of Michigan, also believes that experience can trump biology. Along with psychologist Igor Grossmann, he found that despite a decline in "fluid intelligence" (the mental agility with which we tackle an unfamiliar problem), as we age we tend to get better at complicated reasoning regarding people, ethical issues, or politics.

INTO OUR 70s
THE GOLDEN DECADE?

The happiness U-curve (see p16) continues its upward trajectory in our 70s. For those who have good health and the resilience to overcome any crises, this phase of life could be the rosiest of all.

Accchording to the UN definition, you've already experienced a decade of "old age" when you reach 70 – although it usually doesn't feel that way. People have different views of what constitutes old age, according to their own positioning on the timeline: for example, in a study of 3,000 Americans it was found that those between the ages of 18 and 30 set the start of old age at 60,

whereas subjects aged 65 and over answered 74. One British survey showed that people think of old age beginning in the late 60s; Europeans, on average, set the threshold at 62.

How our lives unfold

These thresholds fail to take into account the actual experience of a life unfolding gradually through time, rather than jumping from one stage to another, as if a border were being crossed. Symbolic moments are massively outnumbered in life by regular moments that don't draw such attention to themselves. This continual gathering of experience and any sense of "mellowing" we might feel in our 70s points to a levelling off of anxiety and

frustration: the most contented people tend to be those who value what's good in their day-to-day experiences rather than fixating on the signs of aging.

Relationships acquire deeper meaning, too, and this, along with a sustaining sense of purpose

> Don't act your age [in retirement]. Act like the **inner young person** you have always been.
>
> **J. A. West**
> Author

Q HASSLE-FREE LIVING?

Carolyn Aldwin, gerontology professor at Oregon State University in the US, has argued that older adults on average have "fewer hassles" – and respond to them better – than younger adults. Until their mid-70s at least, they also "experience more uplifts". After 70, she continues, much depends on how you respond to your issues, and that may be dependent on your resources or your circumstances. It also, of course, depends on your attitude: a positive approach creates a benevolent feedback loop, since others will be inspired by your positivity and you'll feel this in richer relationships.

(which can be anything from grandparenting to volunteering at the local hospital), can make our 70s the happiest decade.

Free at last

If you tease out the strands bundled into happiness, one that stands out at this stage of life is the sense of liberation. With less need than ever to conform, we can rejoice in the freedom to do and say as we please. This doesn't mean pursuing selfish ends regardless of the consequences. Instead, satisfaction is gained from being the unabashed truth-speaker, empathetic to others (since experience can bring great understanding), and tactful if needed, yet willing to offer the fruits of wisdom even when that flies in the face of fashion or convention.

SHARING YOUR 70S

According to a 75-year ongoing Harvard survey of heterosexual couples, our 70s are likely to be a particularly happy time. The study identifies four factors that make it easier for both partners to find a sweet spot of accord:

- The children have left home, which is seen in a positive light.

- Hormonal changes make men and women emotionally and temperamentally more similar.

- Mutual interdependence is seen as a plus rather than a minus.

- The potential trials of dealing with difficult children and aging parents have passed.

ANNIVERSARY GIFT

Given that dissatisfied couples are more likely to divorce, it may not be surprising that the study, left, found that **between the ages of 20 and 70**, only...

18%

...of **both partners described their marriages as happy** for at least 20 years. However, **by the age of 85**...

76%

...of marriages were described as **happy by both partners**.

HAPPY VALLEY: THREE STUDIES

Although many studies of aging focus on declining powers (perhaps because it's easier to measure loss of physical ability, for example, than increased intuition), the three studies below highlight some of the less tangible findings about happiness and our 70s.

Joy in small things
A study published in the *Canadian Medical Association Journal* found that in later life wellbeing depends partly on staying positive and finding joy in small things.

Life-giving friendships
Another study from the Office of National Statistics in the UK has shown that those who spend more time with friends are likely to live longer than those who don't.

Another ordinary day
A third study, published in the *Journal of Consumer Research*, looked at how "extraordinary and ordinary life experiences" influenced happiness. While young people often derive happiness from extraordinary experiences, such as major celebrations, older people derive more happiness from the ordinary things in life.

REACHING OUR 80s

THE NEW 70s

Reaching 80 is a cause for celebration: there's still the possibility of a decade or more of quality living, and your perspective on life will be valued by those who have the good sense to respect experience.

Americans who were asked whether they liked the idea of a hypothetical new president in his or her 80s on balance decided not – but only because of the risk that the candidate wouldn't see out the full term of office with his or her faculties intact. The role of the elder statesman is just one example of the authoritativeness we attribute to someone of advanced years. Diplomacy is one of a number of talents that's enlarged by encountering a wide range of different situations over time. Long memories can have great vocational value.

The wisdom of age

Teaching is another example of an activity that can benefit from decades of practice. While few people in their 80s will be teachers in schools (a significant

10 years

A LONGER LIFE

Research in the US suggests that, on average, you're likely to live **10 years longer than your parents**, and **stay healthier for longer**.

KEEPING AN OPEN MIND

Long before you reach your 80s, examine your own attitude to advanced age. Spend time with seniors you know, talking openly and engaging with what they say. Otherwise, a negative pattern may develop. People who are prejudiced against old age may find that their prejudice turns around and bites them when they find themselves crossing the threshold into that phase of life.

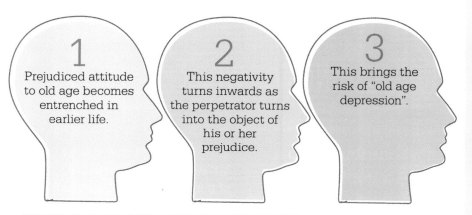

1 Prejudiced attitude to old age becomes entrenched in earlier life.

2 This negativity turns inwards as the perpetrator turns into the object of his or her prejudice.

3 This brings the risk of "old age depression".

minority are, however, active in universities, where longevity of intellect is often prized), many will be valued as sources of wisdom within an *informal* context, such as in the extended family or in the neighbourhood. The idea is still more accepted in tribal or non-Western societies.

All in the mind

Given the obvious impact of health on wellbeing, contentment among those in their 80s often rests on having reliable health care provision. Our sense of security in this respect may depend on where we live, and on our financial circumstances.

Intelligence and memory can remain virtually unchanged in healthy individuals well into their 80s, although cognitive decline

is a serious possibility. So long as you can function mentally, and have some degree of independence (even in care), at 80 you'll be free of the pressure of finding happiness outside yourself: with luck and the right attitude you'll find it inside. You'll no longer be so concerned about your looks, and instead of striving towards some future scenario, you'll have learned to live more in the present.

A natural contentment in simply being may not be enough in itself. But if you can combine that with stimulation and social or intimate contact, you've a good chance of being grateful for your extended lifespan. Reduced energy levels may not matter so much when you no longer have anything to prove or when you have few, if any, pressing deadlines.

THE KEYS TO A LONG LIFE

The secret of a long, healthy life is to be sensible about your lifestyle choices and general outlook. The importance of this has been shown in a study of men who reached 90 or older. Women exhibited less of a correlation in this respect. The study suggested that you:

- Don't smoke.
- Drink in moderation, if at all.
- Follow a healthy diet.
- Stay sociable.
- Manage stress whenever possible.
- Stay positive.
- Cultivate a sense of purpose.
- Be active, mentally and physically.
- Observe safety precautions.
- Have regular health checks.

70 to 90

IN PEAK CONDITION

A **study by Dr Laurel Yates**, at the Brigham and Women's Hospital in Boston, Massachusetts, from the 1980s to 2006, led her to conclude that a man aged 70 has a **54 per cent chance of reaching 90** if he doesn't smoke or have diabetes, has healthy weight and blood pressure, and takes regular exercise. Cutting out the exercise reduces the likelihood to **44 per cent**. The chances reduced further with high blood pressure (**36 per cent**), obesity (**26 per cent**), and smoking (**22 per cent**).

JOBS FOR ALL
THE MEANINGS OF WORK

Meaning at work can come from contributing to a process, from being challenged, and from engaging in purposeful activity. Understanding your relationship with your job will help you deal with its absence.

There's a work *ethic*: the idea that it's morally good for us to work. But there's also a work *instinct*: the use of work to satisfy various psychological needs, quite apart from the practical needs of an income to support ourselves and our family. These needs vary from person to person, and the quality of our retirement, at least initially, will depend to some extent on the particular combination and strength of those needs.

What are your priorities?

Work can serve as a tonic for personal identity, by boosting self-esteem. Meaningful employment can confer a sense of identity, self-worth, and dignity. In achieving satisfactory results, especially when a task is challenging, you may feel that you're realizing more of your potential, and

80,000 hours

PUTTING IN THE TIME

In the US, people spend on average **35–40 hours working** every week. This amounts to about **80,000 hours during a whole career** – potentially more time than they spend with their children.

growing not just as a worker but as a person. This sense of purpose and belonging can become so strong that you may come to see other aspects of life, even your relationships, as secondary to work.

Beyond your control?

When work assumes such a high level of psychological importance in a person's life, they may not necessarily be entirely conscious of the fact. You may believe that you prioritize your family rather than your career, for example, but then something happens that proves otherwise. Usually, this is an instance of conflicting priorities, a moment when you're forced to choose between work and family obligations. Anyone opting for work consistently when presented with dilemmas like this may find that their relationship with a partner, or with friends, starts to fracture.

Q WORK AND POWER

Many kinds of work are empowering in that they provide a domain over which you exert control. The obvious example is the CEO at the head of an organization, but empowerment can come from less elevated roles, too. A long-distance truck driver, for example, might feel liberated in the cab because driving is an autonomous activity and he or she can choose where and when to break the journey. Entrepreneurs often go into business by themselves so they can be their own boss. Many people who have relationship issues at home see work as a liberating environment where they have more power or where communication is better.

Striking the right balance

Work is often experienced as providing a counterbalance to family life, or a relationship, and to other priorities such as leisure time spent with friends. You can get used to this balance, and from that familiarity can grow something approaching dependence. This effect can occur even when the individual *doesn't* find work particularly purposeful – this is an example of finding meaning *at* work rather than *in* work, to use a distinction formulated by organizational experts Michael Pratt and Blake Ashforth. What's valued in such cases is often companionship, routine, a change of environment, and, perhaps subconsciously, a break from domestic life. As with other established patterns in life, giving

WHAT'S IT ALL ABOUT?

In employment, a sense of identity and self-worth comes from two possible sources: the work itself and your relationship with it (work content), and the experience of working with others (work environment). In an ideal world, our work is productive and gives us a sense of purpose, and we gain a sense of belonging from working with colleagues to achieve a common purpose.

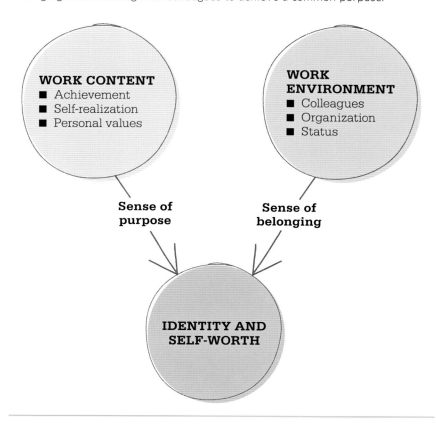

WORK CONTENT
- Achievement
- Self-realization
- Personal values

WORK ENVIRONMENT
- Colleagues
- Organization
- Status

Sense of purpose

Sense of belonging

IDENTITY AND SELF-WORTH

up the work pattern, whatever form this takes, can require a tricky period of adaptation.

Finding silver linings

Unhappiness at work, which can be experienced even by those who have control over their time and workload, often derives from a deeper dissatisfaction with the self. The more self-knowledge you have, therefore, the more adjusted you're

likely to be to your work role. Some people have made friends with their job, others regard it like a relative they don't really like but can't avoid. Excessive expectation is one of the greatest causes of job dissatisfaction; such feelings of potential never realized may continue long after retirement. An honest assessment now will put you in the best position to prepare for the challenges ahead.

ALL TOGETHER

WORK AS COMMUNITY

The workplace is a social and cultural community, with its own traditions and social rituals: we celebrate birthdays, exchange news and views, make leaving speeches, and are sincerely concerned when someone falls ill.

Work also provides the ideal opportunity to participate in a collective endeavour. While a minority of people may find a similar sense of shared purpose in a sports team, for example, for many work is unique in this respect. At home, childcare or running a household has some similar characteristics, too, but with co-workers your relationship is less emotional, and the results of your combined efforts can be measured more easily and over

Having a role within a work group or network, even if we socialize with only some of its members, can be psychologically rewarding and give us a sense of belonging. So what might you miss when you leave?

A HAPPY WORKPLACE?

The factors below, in combination, help make the workplace a peaceful and rewarding environment:

- Respect and politeness shown to all by employer and co-workers.
- Credit given to all for the significance of their contributions.
- Reasonableness valued; antisocial behaviour not tolerated.
- Tolerance of personal difference (eg faith or political affiliation).
- Systems that are flexible enough to accommodate personal needs where appropriate.
- Realistic expectations applied to all by employer and co-workers.

a shorter timeframe. All this gives work a sense of "arm's-length" cooperative enterprise, which many people find rewarding.

Friends or colleagues?

Work politics can be fraught, even in a small group, but sharing a purpose helps to cement bonds of comradeship that can easily turn into friendship. People who spend all day together get to know each other not only from talking socially but also from professional interactions. Difficult times, such as the threat of downsizing, can make bonds even closer.

Solo workers, such as freelancers or self-employed entrepreneurs, may have their own equivalent of work comradeship, in the form of professional entertaining. A client network may not offer the physical proximity of relationships within a single place of work, but it can still be socially rewarding, in ways that people might be sorry to lose in retirement.

Glad or sad to be going?

For all the benefits of a workplace community, the following aspects may make you long for retirement (although you may still miss them once you've left):

- People being openly emotional about work issues (eg loudly resisting necessary changes).
- Workplace politics.
- Poor communication from the employer.

THE BIG SEVEN

Psychologists have identified seven morale-boosting qualities present in the harmonious workplace:

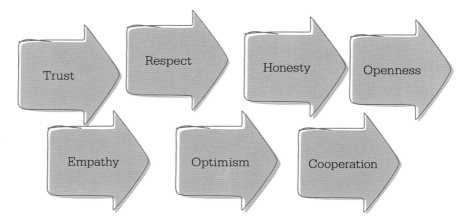

In some work environments, one or more of the following elements work in the opposite direction, lowering morale:

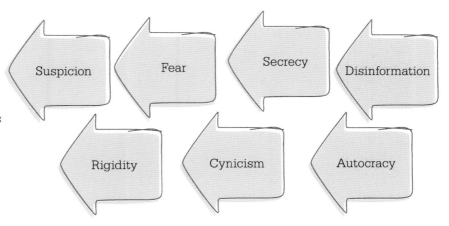

- Attitudes among colleagues that are counter to your personal values.
- Lack of fairness in the way the employer treats the workers.

Older workers may find the workplace rejuvenating, as a result of mixing with younger people. On the other hand, if your colleagues are predominantly youthful, there's a danger of feeling outdated, especially if you sense that age discrimination is in evidence. Having even just one like-minded work friend of a similar age is likely to have a positive effect on your state of mind at work, and if that person leaves before you, it can be a powerful incentive to bring forward your own retirement date.

WHO AM I?

THE QUESTION OF IDENTITY

To choose our best direction in life and the right approach to retirement, it helps if we have an understanding of the roles we perform and the labels other people, perhaps unfairly, attach to us.

When he wrote "I contain multitudes," the American poet Walt Whitman perhaps meant that we should think of ourselves differently in different situations. The question "Who am I?" can become an anxious and important one if we feel that an essential part of ourselves is not being expressed.

The value of values

Our sense of our own identity is partly bound up with our values, which we act on when we make key choices in our lives – for example, our career, relationships, and the way we vote in political elections. Identity, however, is not entirely, or even mostly, a matter of choice. We tend to absorb values from outside ourselves, as a result of social and sometimes parental pressures, and these values will sometimes conflict with what we believe to be our authentic self.

Reading the label

One way in which we might define ourselves, and discover a sense of identity, is through one or more of our roles in life, since it's easier for us to express what we *do* than what we *are*. These two separate things may then become merged. Work roles, especially those that lend themselves to simple labels, such as teacher, manager, cook, stand in for the more complex realities of identity. We'll often identify with other labels, too – for example, parent, daughter, carer, green activist. The more we allow work to dominate our lives, the more our work role identity starts to usurp these other ways of thinking about ourselves.

Life is messy

According to many psychologists, forming an identity is a matter of "finding yourself" by matching your talents and potential with the roles available to you in your social environment. This can be difficult, and people who struggle with the issue may turn to darker identities, such as drinker or gambler, in an attempt to create meaning in their lives. Identity doesn't remain fixed, either, but changes as your life develops. In fact, the most recent theorists claim the self cannot be seen just as a single entity with a solid core. It's counterproductive to seek to "tidy up" the self; better to accept identity's intrinsic messiness and resistance to neat formulations.

True or false?

Many people, at particular times in their lives, attempt to project a false identity that satisfies the expectations of others – an example might be the host of a fund-raising supper who attempts to come over as gregarious and welcoming but in fact is plagued by social anxiety. Attempting to misrepresent yourself like this is stressful and tiring, since the mind is full of self-doubt and

THE FREEDOM TO BE

Some psychologists see self-determination, or free will, as an important human need. We are self-determined when we have a sense of who we are, and how that identity motivates us in the choices we make. Self-determination sets us on the path to optimum function and growth. It is composed of three elements:

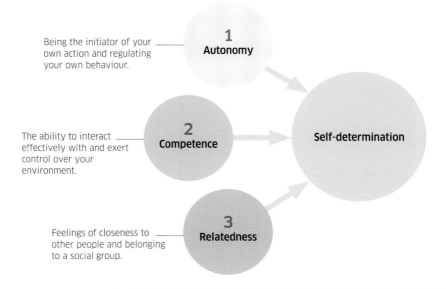

Being the initiator of your own action and regulating your own behaviour.

1 Autonomy

The ability to interact effectively with and exert control over your environment.

2 Competence

Self-determination

Feelings of closeness to other people and belonging to a social group.

3 Relatedness

negativity. Also, there's a risk that you'll start to feel trapped in a life that isn't entirely yours.

Prior to and after retirement the following identities might appear to be available. Be aware that you might feel pressure to adopt one of them, even while you adjust to the changes in your life:

- **Escapee** – delighted to be free of the burden of work.
- **Committed grandparent** – keen to take on family duties.
- **Wise senior** – experienced enough to deal with change.
- **Freelancer** – looking forward to supplementing pension.
- **Adventurous traveller** – able at last to start seeing the world.

FINDING YOUR TRUE SELF

Denying or repressing your true, or authentic, self – the person you believe yourself at heart to be – can damage your prospects of happiness. To live in harmony with your true self, you'll need to try to do the following:

- Locate your personal potential – the things you do best. You can discover this through self-understanding, experiment, and feedback from other people.
- Define your life's purposes – realistically, in ways compatible with your potential.
- Seek opportunities to realize your potential and fulfil the purposes you've chosen for yourself.

MAKING SENSE
LIFE'S MEANING AND PURPOSE

Life feels more meaningful if you're following a purpose. A job is often one of the key purposes of life, giving direction and motivation – but what else allows us to lead fulfilled, meaningful lives?

Generally, meaning follows purpose like a rainbow follows rain. To take a creative activity as an example, purpose and meaning come from the activity itself, while meaning continues beyond the activity, either in the thing created or the memory of an experience.

We all have a psychological need for purpose and meaning in our lives; a sense that our life is greater than the sum of its parts, which in turn improves wellbeing and general happiness levels. A study published in *Psychological Science* in 2014 suggests that "finding a direction for life and setting overarching goals for what you want to achieve" has a significant, positive impact on life expectancy.

What are my purposes now?

Thinking about how and where we find purpose and meaning in our lives can help maintain or improve our wellbeing during the transition to retirement. It's vital for our psychological health to be able to assess and set our own directions.

Try making a list of the activities or goals that give you a sense of meaning or contentedness. These could be anything from spending time with family or friends to painting, playing sport, finishing a task, practising a craft, being part of a committee, or reading a book. Having a clear idea of what makes you happy now will give you a sense of how things will change once you're out of employment.

Finding meaning

We tend to find meaning through two different channels: purposeful activity and valuable experiences. The former is future-oriented, in that we create goals to aim for, which give us a sense of purpose; career progression may be our key purpose for many years. The latter is more experiential; friendships, relationships, and family all fall into this latter

THE FOUNDATIONS OF PURPOSE

- **Health** – good physical and mental wellbeing reduces the likelihood of ill health and lets you focus on goals and experiences that matter.

- **Independence** – it's vital to have control over at least some areas of your life in order to determine your own aims and purposes.

- **Interdependence** – a sense of connectedness with others provides you with a safe environment from which to pursue your life aims.

THE VALUE OF MEANING

Martin Seligman, the pioneer of positive psychology, defines the meaningful life as knowing what your best qualities are and "using your signature strengths and virtues in the service of something much larger than you are." The meaningful life forms one of three dimensions of happiness, along with the good life and the pleasant life.

THE MEANINGFUL LIFE
Finding your unique strengths and employing them for a purpose greater than yourself.

THE GOOD LIFE
Discovering what you're good at and applying these skills to worthwhile pursuits.

A HAPPY LIFE

THE PLEASANT LIFE
Enjoying basic pleasures such as companionship, nature, and intimacy.

category, as does appreciation of sensory stimulation, such as taking pleasure in the natural world.

Changing purposes

People who see themselves as having a vocation – as many doctors and actors do, to take just two examples – can often express their purpose in life with relative ease, even though they may well experience periods of self-doubt. Others, who are less committed to a particular career path, may look for purpose outside work. In between are the many people who are ambivalent about their career, and seek a clear sense of purpose there with little success.

It's important to assess how closely your sense of purpose is associated with your job; those who are inclined to find meaning elsewhere are more likely to experience the transition to retirement as a positive change, allowing them to spend more time on the things they already love, whereas those who are dedicated to their work may take longer to adjust. Regardless of your position, it's a good idea to prioritize those non-work-related, meaningful activities *before* you retire. Allowing these activities to take up more space in your life will ease the transition. "Practising" your retirement in this way will allow you to make the practical and psychological adjustments necessary to promote happiness during retirement.

WE MAKE A LIVING BY WHAT WE GET WE MAKE A LIFE BY WHAT WE GIVE

WINSTON CHURCHILL
STATESMAN, ORATOR, AND AUTHOR

MATERIAL WORLD
PERSPECTIVES ON MONEY

People often pursue money to "improve" their lifestyle, but it can take on a symbolic value that colours our self-image. Getting money in perspective can help you deal with reduced income in retirement.

Money can cause problems in life – not only when you don't have enough to house, feed, and clothe yourself and your family. The term "affluenza" (see opposite) has been coined to describe one of the sicknesses of consumerism, symptomized by debt, waste, and anxiety, resulting from a narrow focus on acquiring wealth.

Naked ambition

The idea that wealth, like power, corrupts, though contradicted by examples of philanthropy and charitable works, does seem to have some truth to it. Uninherited wealth often stems from ambition, which operates in a competitive arena: the image of the ruthless financier is well known in popular

25%

DOES MONEY MATTER?
According to a 2013 LifeTwist study, **only about 25 per cent** of people in the US regard money as an **indication of success**.

THE CURSE OF "AFFLUENZA"?

Living the dream? Not necessarily. A lifestyle funded largely by debt makes you susceptible to changes in the economy, such as rising interest rates. The more finely tuned your debt-income ratio, the more vulnerable you are.

Debt makes you dependent on:	Major costs of a high-end lifestyle include:
■ Employment, and possibly wage inflation. ■ Buying on credit. ■ Moderate interest rates so that debt repayments never become unaffordable.	■ Private school fees. ■ Private health insurance. ■ Home renovation. ■ Entertaining. ■ Expensive holidays.

culture. However, in an age when immorality in business is more closely scrutinized than ever, ruthlessness no longer has the survival value it once did.

Addicted to money?

People whose morals remain uncorrupted by money may still be at the mercy of compulsive behaviour. Psychologist Dr Tian Dayton has identified the need to acquire money as one of the so-called process or behavioural addictions, alongside gambling, sex, and eating. A shift takes place in the chemistry of the brain so that money produces a detectable "high".

You can't buy happiness

There's no doubt that not having an adequate supply of money closes many doors in life. However, it's worth noting that once you have enough money

to support a modest lifestyle, greater wealth has no effect on wellbeing or contentment. The culprit behind this finding is not money in itself, but the ambitious striving for it, which attacks peace of mind and may damage relationships. Fortunately, the link between money and success is breaking down, as people look outside this realm for their sources of satisfaction.

 RECIPE FOR WEALTH

The following life choices and approaches to life are most conducive to becoming wealthy:

■ Making the right career choice.
■ Living below your means.
■ Prioritizing your time efficiently to increase your chances of making money.
■ Valuing financial independence above social status.

WEALTH AND EMPATHY

Research published in the journal *Psychological Science* reveals that people of lower economic status are more skilled at reading facial expressions than wealthier people. These skills might be more important in the world in which they operate. Co-author Michael Kraus says that lower-status individuals have to respond to various social threats, and so hone their empathy skills to be able to detect dangers accurately, and to cooperate with others in defending their communities.

WEALTH AND MORALITY

Wealth may even compromise moral judgment. A study conducted by the University of California, Berkeley, found that in San Francisco, where it's a legal requirement for cars to stop at intersections to allow pedestrians to cross the road, those driving expensive cars were four times less likely to conform. Another study (conducted at Harvard and the University of Utah) showed that simply thinking about words related to money seems to make subjects more likely to lie or behave immorally afterwards.

DOES STATUS MATTER?

STEPPING OFF THE CAREER LADDER

Career progress over a working life often brings status. Being aware of where you got your sense of status from at work will help you prepare for a potential loss of status in retirement.

The exact meaning of job status varies greatly according to context. In low-employment cultures, for example, simply *having* a job might be a major source of prestige. Elsewhere, your job sector may play a part – you might belong to a respected profession, for example, or work for a company with a proud culture. Status can also be reflected in your job role, with job titles acting as milestones along the way to personal achievement. When a word like "senior" or "chief" is included, this may be felt as a badge of status rather than merely indicating function. In fact, it's common for people to relish the implications of the level they've reached without always being able to identify what matters to them most. In this way, status may be subliminally valuable as part of your self-image.

Staying flexible

These interpretations of status are likely to be less relevant to you if you have followed a flexible career pattern – moving from company to company, gathering new experiences and skills, say, rather than upwards within the same organization. With this type of "boundaryless" career (a term coined by Professor Michael B. Arthur and others in the late 1990s), status is defined by your own criteria – such as a sense of personal growth – rather than being dependent on an employer's assessment of your worth.

THE TRIANGLE OF STATUS
Your standing in society - or socioeconomic status (SES) - can be measured as a combination of three factors (shown here). Each can contribute to a deeply felt sense of self.

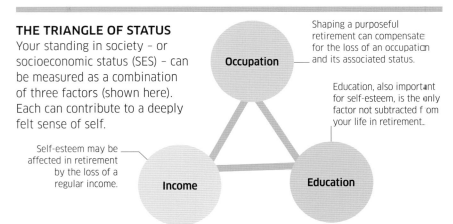

Self-esteem may be affected in retirement by the loss of a regular income.

Shaping a purposeful retirement can compensate for the loss of an occupation and its associated status.

Education, also important for self-esteem, is the only factor not subtracted from your life in retirement.

Occupation

Income

Education

⑦ WHAT DOES STATUS LOOK LIKE?

You can find status at work in any or all of the following areas:

- Your level of responsibility or autonomy.
- Your job title.
- Your membership of a board or management group.
- The number of people reporting to you.
- Your role in representing the company or organization to others.
- Symbolic aspects – such as the size of your desk or office, or whether you have a parking space.
- Your salary and fringe benefits.

Working well

If you make a work contribution that others, as well as yourself, value it can be a tonic for your personal identity and self-esteem, putting you in a positive frame of mind for retirement. However, the more rooted your self-esteem is in your job, the more likely you are to find retirement a challenge.

If this sounds like you, it's important to plan your retirement with this in mind, retaining a link with your "old" working identity. A phased retirement (see pp82–83) can help smooth the transition, for example. Alternatively, setting up as a consultant in your field of expertise (see pp84–85) can allow you to reinvent your sense of self by building successful past experiences into your life plan.

SATISFACTION GUARANTEED?

American psychologist Professor Paul E. Spector, who conducted a major study on the subject in the 1990s, divides job satisfaction into 14 categories, listed below along with some aspects you might miss in retirement.

Category	In retirement you might miss...
1 **Appreciation**	The value placed on your contribution – the thanks expressed.
2 **Recognition**	Being seen as significant, with a clearly defined role.
3 **Job conditions**	The work environment, infrastructure, location, décor, and desk.
4 **Pay**	A regular salary, which you might miss even if you have a generous pension.
5 **Organization**	The sense of working within a clear, functional structure.
6 **Promotion**	The sense of progressing up a career ladder and your achievements being recognized.
7 **Supervision**	Your boss's regard for your contribution. (A lack of supervision might also be a *positive* factor.)
8 **Fringe benefits**	Your company car, for example, or free gym membership.
9 **Performance-based rewards**	Recognition of your achievements in the form of bonuses or similar rewards.
10 **Operating procedures**	The pleasure taken in the smooth running of systems, to which you may contribute.
11 **Security**	A sense of belonging, making a contribution over time, and a degree of protection from change.
12 **Co-workers**	Companionship and respect; your status among your colleagues.
13 **Nature of work**	Exercising a skill or competence; a sense of purpose; a sense of making a social contribution.
14 **Communication**	Cooperation, teamwork, and dialogue.

ARE YOU A WORKAHOLIC?

WHEN YOUR JOB IS YOUR LIFE

Some of us like our jobs, some of us love our jobs – and some of us don't know how to live without our jobs. If your job has been everything to you, how do you cope with impending retirement?

Is "workaholic" really the best word to use: surely work isn't addictive? Actually, according to recent research, the term might be more appropriate than we think.

Heavily invested or hooked?

Being a workaholic is not necessarily psychologically unhealthy. A 2012 paper in *Human Resource Management Review* makes a distinction between two types of workaholics called Heavy Work Investors (HWI): situational HWI – someone who works hard because they have to; and dispositional HWI – someone who doesn't have to make their job their life, but does so anyway. It's useful to consider where you fit in (see opposite): people who are dispositionally HWI may well need more support when it comes to retirement.

A serious addiction?

Can you get literally addicted to your job? Writer Johann Hari argues in *Chasing the Scream* that first we need to consider how addiction works. In the 1970s, Canadian psychologist Bruce Alexander started picking holes in the traditional lab-rat studies of addiction. True, those rats chose drugged water over clean – but given their sterile, lonely cages, there wasn't much else for them to do but get high. Alexander built new cages with toys, tunnels, food, and other rats for company, and found that the rats could take

HOW HOOKED ON WORK ARE YOU?

Are all busy workers workaholics? Not according to Israeli researchers Raphael Snir and Itzhak Harpaz, who argue that there are shades of grey to do with circumstances and temperament. Do any of the types below sound like you?

Situational Heavy Work Investor	Dispositional Heavy Work Investor	
■ **Type 1 – The needy**: those who have a big family to feed, debts to pay, etc. ■ **Type 2 – The employer-directed**: those who work in environments such as hospitals, where the hours are high for everyone.	■ **Type 1 – Workaholics**: those with a genuine addiction-type relationship to their work. ■ **Type 2 – The work-devoted**: those whose job is their consuming passion.	■ **Type 3 – Intimacy-avoiders**: those who flee from relationships into work. ■ **Type 4 – The leisure-low-interested**: those who are bored "doing nothing" and work to keep themselves occupied.

or leave the drugged water. With other sources of comfort, the rats didn't get addicted.

Addiction or bonding?

Psychology professor Peter Cohen has argued that "addiction" is the wrong word: a more accurate one would be "bonding". In a healthy life, we bond with people around us: that's where we get our psychological rewards. But if that doesn't work out, we can bond with other things, such as drugs, gambling, and work.

If you think you fit that compulsive profile, retirement may pose a challenge and you'd be well advised to seek help first. It's all too easy to replace one compulsion with another, and the last thing you need is to spend your retirement fighting another kind of addiction.

THE DISLOCATION THEORY OF ADDICTION

Psychologist Bruce Alexander argues that it's not chemicals that hook us, but a world in which we're "dislocated" from real connection. He presents it as an unhappy circle:

A society that's fragmented rather than supportive.

People grow dislocated from meaningful connections.

Flood of addictions – drugs, wealth, gambling, career, etc.

Consequences of addictions: society grows colder and less stable.

A LIFE OF VALUES
BEYOND BASIC NEEDS

We all carry around a set of values, which motivate our decisions and affect every aspect of our lives. Identifying your values now will help you shape a meaningful new life when you retire.

Values affect our attitudes and behaviour, and act as a compass as we navigate a path through life. They can influence our decisions, affect our actions and opinions, and determine our priorities.

Where do they come from?
Values can be intuitive or reasoned, and we gather them throughout our lives. The process starts early: if one of your parents was an artist, for example, you might place a high premium on creativity; or if you grew up in an industrial town, you might value labour or enterprise. These intuitive or "inherited" values tend to be fixed over a lifetime. Other values we choose consciously through reasoning,

framing and adjusting them on the basis of our personal experiences or considered thought.

Conflict of interest
Sometimes the way we live our lives is in conflict with our values, and this can become a source of tension and stress. For example, you might work for a company that, contrary to your values, puts profit above people, or uses selling techniques you don't agree with. Or perhaps you have a high regard for family life but find yourself having to work long hours or unsociable shifts. In such circumstances, most of us try to organize our lives so that we can be true to our values, perhaps with some self-sacrifice, but it isn't always possible.

Time well spent?
Making the effort to identify your values helps you make key decisions in life. A major aspect of this relates to how you spend your time, including your work-life balance. Identifying your own value system (see opposite) can be a revealing measure of how your values match your life right now, and which areas you might need to address in retirement.

? PUTTING IT INTO PRACTICE

As you approach retirement, values will help inform your priorities in life, providing answers to questions such as:

- Shall I spend more time with children and grandchildren?
- Shall I be a carer for elderly parents?
- Shall I work as a volunteer?
- Shall I campaign on local issues?
- Shall I start a small business?
- Shall I take over some of my partner's household duties?

IDENTIFYING YOUR VALUES

Values matter – after all, if everyone followed the same values, there would be no politics, debates, or wars. To identify what's important to you, try sketching out your own value system, which may look something like the diagram below. Either create your own categories or follow the ones given here. Vary the size of the outer spheres depending on how much importance you place on certain areas of your life.

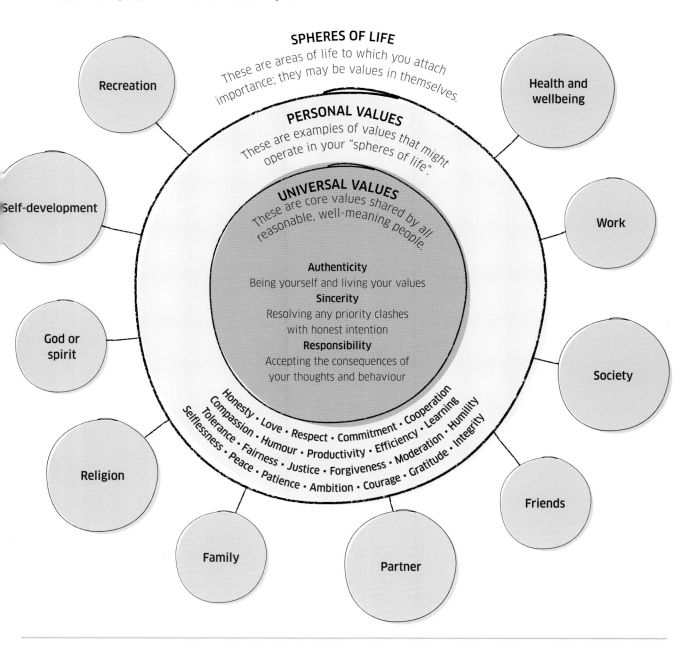

SPHERES OF LIFE
These are areas of life to which you attach importance; they may be values in themselves.

PERSONAL VALUES
These are examples of values that might operate in your "spheres of life".

UNIVERSAL VALUES
These are core values shared by all reasonable, well-meaning people.

Authenticity
Being yourself and living your values
Sincerity
Resolving any priority clashes with honest intention
Responsibility
Accepting the consequences of your thoughts and behaviour

Honesty · Love · Respect · Commitment · Cooperation
Compassion · Humour · Productivity · Efficiency · Learning · Humility
Tolerance · Fairness · Justice · Forgiveness · Moderation · Integrity
Selflessness · Peace · Patience · Ambition · Courage · Gratitude

Recreation

Self-development

God or spirit

Religion

Family

Partner

Friends

Society

Work

Health and wellbeing

THE ROAD TO SOMEWHERE
THE IMPORTANCE OF LIFE GOALS

In your career, goal-setting can be part of the formula for success. But how important is it in other areas of your life as you pursue happiness and wellbeing, and how can it help as you plan for retirement?

Some companies are cautious about setting precise goals, since a more open-minded approach can increase a company's ability to respond to market factors. It's true that one of the difficulties with goal-setting is that circumstances can change in ways beyond your control and make your goals obsolete. However, as long as you take a flexible approach – setting goals, but not in concrete – you're likely to find them useful as orientation points in your life. They give you a sense of purpose, which satisfies an important psychological need. That, in turn, gives you guidance in how to manage your time, establish your priorities, and plan your vision of the future.

Goals... or limitations?

Defining your goals can mean defining your limitations, putting you on a narrow course that might result in you missing out on many opportunities in life. Having achieved your goal, you can tick a particular box: but perhaps you'll never know about other, more worthwhile boxes that you could have ticked if you'd taken a more open, improvising approach. It certainly makes sense, when goal-setting, to focus on the process rather than the outcome and to review your goals on a regular basis.

Aim for a range

Having a range of goals over all areas of your life, pursued with flexibility, can be deeply enriching. You might, for example, be ambitious in different ways for your health and wellbeing, relationship, family life, friendships, finances, leisure time, and personal projects. Any disappointments will be less overwhelming if you balance your energies in this way, and you'll have a better sense of yourself as a well-rounded, versatile individual acting in harmony with others.

100%

THE ARITHMETIC OF PROGRESS

If you commit today to making a **1-per-cent improvement on a daily basis**, in 68 days' time you'll be **100-per-cent better** than you were yesterday.

A purposeful retirement

If you balance your ambitions in this way before retirement, you'll be less likely to feel the shock of work goals suddenly evaporating, since other areas of your life will already be full of purpose. Retirement is a wonderful opportunity to set new goals, but some people do this to conform to the modern image of the contented retiree – in other words, out of peer pressure – rather than as the authentic expression of a passion. Trying to conjure up goals from scratch is a recipe for unhappiness. Start with your interests and see where they take you, allowing goals to evolve, at least to embryo stage. Show some self-compassion, too – if initial experiments come to nothing, you've got plenty of time now to find goals that suit you best.

☀ THE ART OF "KAIZEN"

A gradualist approach to goal-setting often works best. Let's say that, in retirement, you decide you're going to learn a new language well enough to be able to hold a conversation during a planned post-retirement trip in a year's time. This puts pressure on you, which in turn may make you less motivated. It would be better to make an indefinite commitment to gradual improvement (known in Japanese as "kaizen"), without worrying how fluent you'll be when your trip comes around.

DREAMS INTO GOALS

Once you've established a goal, you need to draw up a plan to test it and put it into action: otherwise, it's merely a dream. The following stages of analysis can be helpful in turning intangible dreams into defined goals:

INTANGIBLE DREAM

Define your goal
- What goal are you setting? Give it a name.
- Does it make sense?
- Does your goal conflict with any of your roles or values?

Set a timeframe
- Do you have an approximate timeframe for realizing your goal?
- How much time will you need to set aside, and when?
- What changes do you need to make to free up this time?

Are you commited?
- How important to you is your goal?
- Do you need to sacrifice anything to make it possible?
- Do you need a period of experiment or research before you fully commit?

What will you need?
- What personal resources will you need to complete your goal?
- Can you rely on them?
- What do you need to do to realize your goal?

Stay flexible
- Which features of your goal are fixed and which are flexible?
- Can you envisage any changes?
- Can you forsee any change in circumstances that might require you to modify your goal?

DEFINED GOAL

THE MEANING OF SERVICE

RESPECT AND REWARD

Being appreciated helps us feel good about ourselves. In retirement, you may miss the respect gained for your purposeful contribution in the workplace, but there are other sources of validation.

In employment, your performance is usually measured objectively. For example, appraisals may be given, formally or informally. In many sectors, achievements can also be quantified in terms of output, budget control, sales figures, or new customer numbers. Increasingly, assessments of satisfaction are sought from consumers. All these measures, when positive, are likely to give you a sense of your own performance, and might be a source of professional pride.

Feeling that you belong

In the workplace, you're likely to earn respect if you make a valuable contribution. This might be reflected in your job title, the degree of responsibility and trust extended to you, and your salary. Respect may also be channelled into words of appreciation – for example, after you've completed a project or solved a challenging problem. In these ways you gain a sense of purpose (see pp28–29). People know what you can offer and come to you to ask for it, which often translates into a sense of belonging, of being a cog happily working in a productive machine.

Being appreciated

If you identify yourself with your work role, that identification is likely to be reinforced if you feel that others appreciate you. Such

THE LEVELS OF RESPECT

In the workplace there are three ways in which respect for your contribution tends to be expressed. These are detailed below, with possible equivalents that you might find in retirement.

DEFERENCE FROM PEOPLE BELOW YOUR LEVEL

In work this may be accompanied by admiration, and gratitude for your mentoring.

In retirement you could find this by nurturing and tutoring the young.

ACCEPTANCE AND RECOGNITION FROM YOUR PEERS

In work this may be accompanied by comradeship, solidarity, or friendship.

In retirement you could find this in friendships or family.

ACKNOWLEDGMENT FROM PEOPLE ABOVE YOUR LEVEL

In work this may be accompanied by trust and rewarded by privileges, promotion, bonuses, or salary increases.

In retirement you could find this in an adult education class, for example, by earning the respect of your teacher.

appreciation may be fondly expressed in a leaving speech on the day you retire, poignantly underlining what you'll be missing. Empathetic friends and family may take the trouble in your first months of retirement to express the ways *they* appreciate you, in the domestic or social sphere. Even so, you should expect that you'll need time to adjust to the loss of a clearly defined work role that gave you a sense of service in a larger cause.

A sense of relief?

Many people feel undervalued at work by the people who matter – and this can lead to anxiety. They may feel relief when retirement comes, complicated by an overall sense of failure: the feeling that they never got the chance to prove themselves may rankle for years, undermining their wellbeing. For the self-employed, any validation of purpose may need to come from clients, customers, and other outsiders: for people who work in this way, retirement may be less of a culture shock.

One key to a successful transition is to plan your retirement in a way that gives you identifiable sources of purpose and ensures that your world is broadening rather than narrowing. Having completed your contribution to work, it's time to enlarge your contribution to your personal and family life, and to develop any projects that appeal to you.

THE PURPOSE OF PURPOSE

Serving a purpose makes us less susceptible to boredom, anxiety, and depression. This is because:

- We have an external focus for our attention and are therefore less likely to allow space for negative "mental chatter".
- Following a purpose makes us feel less selfish. It allows us to see our problems in a wider perspective.
- We have the chance of entering a state of "flow" – a complete absorption in a task, to the point of not being aware of time passing. The more flow we experience, the greater our sense of wellbeing.
- Purpose boosts our self-confidence, which feeds into our self-esteem and gives us a sense of hopefulness.

RAINBOW'S END?

THE RETIREMENT DREAM

The future seldom turns out exactly as you envisaged. This can be true of retirement, especially if you see it as a reward for hard work. Instead, try thinking cf retirement as a chance to lead a new, busy life.

Outside the employment context, "retirement" means withdrawal, with overtones of giving up. Yet retirement as a life stage means, for many of us, the prospect of a fresh start, thanks in part to improvements in life expectancy and health care. Typically, we may have 15 to 20 years of quality living ahead of us when we retire.

A blank canvas?

Anyone pursuing greater levels of happiness might see retirement as a blank canvas on which to paint their masterpiece: the final picture, excelling all previous efforts. Unencumbered by work, you have the chance to design your own life's golden age, pursuing new goals, with new purpose, exploring neglected areas of your potential, and realizing either long-cherished ambitions or plans concocted specifically for this "dream time".

What's in a word?

A dream is by definition insubstantial – something that eludes your grasp when you reach out to touch it. A better word might be "vision", since that implies not a wish but a plan: an intention you can realize if you apply yourself in the right way. However, even "vision" may not be quite appropriate to many of us, since it implies something grandiose and utopian. Having a plan – a flexible and multistranded one – might not seem quite so exciting, but may be a more realistic way to think of your future, and one that's less likely to result in disappointment.

Fuelling your dreams

Whatever we call it, a dream (or vision or plan) is the way we like to imagine ourselves in retirement – as long as we stay healthy and can afford to put our plans into action. The reality may be very different, since our projections of the future almost always miss the mark, and also because the practical difficulties involved in attaining a new life may turn out to be insuperable. However, there's no doubt that an image of optimum retirement – the rainbow's end – is highly motivating. A good rule of thumb is to pursue your dream if it corresponds with your passion. A dream on its own, without the fuel of passion to bring it closer, will remain forever intangible.

65-plus

THE QUALITY OF (LATER) LIFE

A 2014 Gallup-Healthways **survey of 85,145 adults** in the US tracked wellbeing in five areas of life. It found that in every area, **people aged 65-plus** reported a **better quality of life** than younger individuals.

TIPPING THE SCALES

The secret to viewing retirement in a positive light is to make the most of new opportunities, grasping them wholeheartedly, rather than drifting into aimless leisure – a dream that can quickly turn sour.

POSITIVE VIEW
- An exciting new stage of life.
- An escape from work politics, and more time for friends.
- Finding new purposes.
- A liberation of your time.
- Retirement as an opportunity to address domestic issues.
- Reduced expenses.

NEGATIVE VIEW
- A difficult time of adjustment.
- Will I miss the company of my work colleagues?
- Losing purposeful employment.
- Losing reassuring routines.
- Work as an escape from domestic issues.
- Reduced income.

AVOIDING RETIREMENT'S PITFALLS

Below are some of retirement's psychological and practical pitfalls. You can avoid many of the practical issues by planning ahead, while simply being aware of the psychological issues will be a big help as you adjust to retirement.

Psychological pitfalls	Practical pitfalls
■ Imagining your first months of retirement will feel liberating and happy.	■ Having too many interests that are expensive to pursue.
■ Believing that inactive leisure is rewarding.	■ Not accurately forecasting your retirement spending.
■ Thinking work colleagues will automatically stay in touch.	■ Not planning adequately for healthcare costs.
■ Believing a new project will be rewarding from the beginning.	■ Believing you can make up for lost investment time.

STAYING BUSY
A SATISFYING RETIREMENT

Feeling connected is the key to happiness, and a satisfying retirement is often one where you make the most of relationships, and forge new ones. Keeping busy creates purpose and prevents boredom, too.

If you're blessed with reasonable health, you'll probably want to be active in retirement, since activity is the essence of a fulfilled life. The chance to be active in your own chosen way is often more welcome than the thought of a well-deserved rest after a life of service. In any case, service – to others you know or to your community – can remain part of a balanced life in retirement, providing a valuable sense of purpose.

Making a contribution
The life experience you'll have gathered during several decades of adulthood is the perfect platform for making a social contribution in all sorts of ways. You're ideally placed to be a mentor, for example. The precise form this takes can range from giving informal advice to younger friends, or children or grandchildren of contemporary friends, to conducting formal training sessions – perhaps in the skills you were employed to use, and possibly even for your old employer. You might want to consider reciprocal mentoring – for example, training a younger person in gardening or childcare, while they in return help you hone your computer skills. All this is a modern interpretation of the ancient role, in traditional village communities, of the elder – the local go-to person for wisdom.

SPHERES OF ACTIVITY

Retirement activities are numerous and varied, but most will sit under one of the headings below. A satisfying retirement will come from pursuing a range of activities under several of these headings. Some activities will be appropriate to more than one heading: for example, a reading group would sit under both "relationships" and "learning".

Learning:
- Practical skills
- Knowledge

Relationships:
- Friends
- Partner

Employment:
- Paid work
- Voluntary work

Caring:
- Parent or other adults
- Grandchildren

Physical:
- Keeping fit
- Team sports

Mentoring:
- Professional knowledge/skills
- Life experience

Making and fixing:
- Home and garden
- Elsewhere

Travel:
- Domestically
- Overseas

Mind and body

A balanced and busy retirement will include ways of keeping fit, through exercise, and having plenty to engage and challenge the mind – anything from daily sudoku or games such as chess or bridge to forming a debating circle, attending lectures, or reading about philosophy or science. Research has found that keeping the brain active appears to increase its vitality and may build reserves of brain cells and new connections: you could even generate new brain cells. Friendships satisfy an obvious emotional need, but you shouldn't forget that they can be mentally or even intellectually stimulating too. There's no better mental exercise than engaging in a friendly disagreement about politics or a point of principle.

Following your passion

Being curious, and following your curiosity can lead you down fascinating paths that, before you know it, become part of your retirement's activity pattern. In employment you may not have time to follow cues in this way, with no idea of where they might lead, but in retirement you'll be ideally placed to explore.

KEEPING THE NETWORK

Staying involved with others is psychologically important at every stage of life. In retirement, you may miss the complex interactions of work, in which case making the most of – and extending – your personal network of family and friends will be vital for your wellbeing. Interpersonal connections not only strengthen your sense of identity and self-worth, but also act as a conduit for all kinds of new interests. It works both ways: following your interests leads you to new people; new people lead you to new interests, as well as new perspectives on established interests.

SENIOR MOMENTS?
TRUTHS AND MYTHS OF AGING

We're regularly confronted with less than positive myths about aging, but recent psychological research confounds such views, providing us with a much brighter outlook on retirement.

The popular image of aging depicts a scenario we might find depressing – if it were true. We think of minds and bodies declining and of life inevitably becoming less rewarding, productive, and enjoyable. Cognitive decline, according to this picture, is inevitable, adding to the prospect of failing physical powers. However, the reality for many of us is, fortunately, quite different.

Feeling your age?
According to Professor Timothy Salthouse, a psychologist at the University of Virginia, "The story used to be that satisfaction with life went downhill, but the remarkable thing that researchers are finding is that doesn't seem to be the case." Some evidence is starting to point to the possibility that, in average terms, our general sense of wellbeing may improve with age.

As for declining mental faculties, experts are finding that knowledge and particular kinds of intelligence continue to develop in a way that may offset age-related declines in our ability to process new information and apply reason logically. Expertise in a subject deepens, which can have the effect of improving productivity and creativity. The old idea of the wise elder, who brings experience to bear to solve a range of problems, is not so far from the truth. Moreover, engaging

Q MISLEADING RESEARCH?

As we get older, our brains take longer to process and retrieve information from our memories. However, older adults who are showing no symptoms of dementia tend to do better in the real world than their performance in scientific cognitive tests would suggest. Scientists tend to favour tests in which past experience plays no part; whereas in reality, much of our mental performance is based on the knowledge we've acquired over time. It's also possible that older people don't feel entirely at ease in lab conditions – especially when compared with the students scientists tend to recruit to represent the younger generation.

the brain in learning new skills – anything from woodworking to trying out the latest gadget – can play a greater part in keeping you mentally sharp as you get older than simply applying skills from your existing repertoire.

Challenges and rewards

This is not to underestimate the challenges of aging. The truth is that fortune treats some of us better than others, even if we've done our best to lead a healthy lifestyle. In later life, chronic conditions such as diabetes, hypertension, and dementia become increasingly common and can seriously undermine wellbeing. Even so, we should resist the tendency to treat worst-case scenarios as the norm.

Bereavement, you might imagine, has a major effect on the outlook of the older generation, perhaps encouraging a tendency towards depression. In fact, depression is perhaps slightly less prevalent in old age than at other times of life (see below). Human beings are impressively resilient in emotional terms, and can often cope with loss, ill-health, and other age-related setbacks with amazing vitality of spirit. Even many centenarians have been shown to remain positive.

One reason for such surprising outcomes is that older adults in general tend to focus on positive rather than negative emotions, and therefore can see the good in less than ideal situations. They are also extremely adaptive to new circumstances.

5.5%

AGING HAPPILY

Seniors seem to be **more content than younger people**. According to the National Institute of Mental Health, 5.5 per cent of adults in the US aged 50 and over said they had had a major depressive episode in 2012. For people aged 26 to 49, the rate was 7.6 per cent; and for the 18-to-25 group it was 8.9 per cent.

Q OLDER AND WISER?

In studies that asked people to nominate individuals they deemed to be wise, the average age for nominees was 55–60, as reported by the psychologist Robert Sternberg. We clearly see some correlation between wisdom and age. One of the earliest considerations of this connection was proposed in 1950 by the psychologist Erik Erikson, who described in his theory of the human life cycle how elderly people struggle to achieve a balance between their personal sense of integrity on the one hand, and defeat by declining powers and mortality on the other. When integrity wins the battle, the consequence is wisdom.

We might define wisdom as the ability to show sound judgment in complex, dynamic situations. Its components involve being able to overcome the sense of self-interest, invulnerability, omniscience, or ominipotence that can characterize lesser forms of intelligence. The wise person is fully self-aware, and conscious of his or her limitations, as well as the best interests of the wider community.

FREE TIME
HOW WE THINK OF LEISURE

In retirement you can be as busy as you ever were, on a range of activities. Building time in your week for hobbies and interests can bring you enhanced wellbeing and various health benefits.

After they've retired, much of the time people once spent working is translated into leisure time – even though this doesn't necessarily represent the best model to aspire to in retirement. According to a recent American Time Use Survey, people aged 65–74 spent an average of seven hours per day on leisure activities, compared to just over five hours among the total adult population.

Blurred edges
"Leisure", however, is a leaky concept – an imprecision that may not be recognized in surveys. "Classic" leisure activities include sports, travel, social activities, and outdoor recreation, but some of these may be done dutifully rather than recreationally – for example, doing light exercise at the gym or visiting a sick relative. Then again, an activity such as shopping – not a traditional leisure activity – is for many highly enjoyable. Equally, projects and volunteering may fall outside the leisure category, even if you find them more rewarding than, say, your weekly bridge session.

Busy doing nothing?
To equate leisure with relaxation, or doing not very much at all, is perfectly acceptable. However, taking this form of leisure as the principal benefit of retirement is likely to lead to disappointment: the luxury quickly palls. Doing nothing is hugely valued when you're working hard, but is hardly a sustainable lifestyle choice, unless you need to take it easy for medical reasons. That said, there's certainly a place in a balanced retirement for physically undemanding pursuits, such as watching TV, reading, and

GOING ONLINE
Social media can open up your possibilities for **leisure and friendships** – you could seek out volunteering opportunities, for example. A 2014 Pew Research Center **survey of internet users** in the US found that...

65%
...of those **aged 50–64 used social media**, compared with...

49%
...of those **aged 65-plus**.

HEALTH BENEFITS OF LEISURE

Hobbies and leisure activities can make an important contribution to health and wellbeing among the 60-plus population, refreshing both mind and body. Research has shown that doing active things we enjoy can help delay the signs of aging and give some degree of protection against certain illnesses. In particular, they can help to:

■ Strengthen the immune system.

■ Improve flexibility.

■ Enhance memory and brain power.

■ Reduce stress.

■ Improve self-esteem.

■ Promote better sleep.

? WHAT DOES LEISURE MEAN?

Leisure can be measured in three different ways: as a state of mind, as a period of time, and as a type of activity:

STATE OF MIND
This is a subjective definition in which leisure is measured as **any activity that is freely chosen**, self-motivated, pleasurable, or emotionally rewarding.

TIME
Leisure can be measured as **residual time**, after work, obligations, and essential tasks such as eating and sleeping are removed from the day.

ACTIVITY
Leisure can also be measured as the **activities we engage in during our free time**, for various reasons such as relaxation, competition, or personal growth. This definition is problematic, since it takes no account of how you feel about such activities.

listening to music. These are passive in the sense of being sedentary, but can be as challenging intellectually as you choose to make them. Dozing in the shade in a recliner on a sunny day brings pleasurable sensations, and a chance to appreciate the outdoors, and any guilt you might feel should be dismissed as an irrelevance. There may be jobs to do, but one of the joys of retirement is that they don't have to be fitted into a narrow time window: so overcome any scruples, relax, and enjoy!

Trying something new

New leisure activities can add an enjoyable dimension to retirement. Some of us, even in retirement,

have a craving for varied, novel, and complex sensations. It's worth considering the physical dimension when you make your selection. Many activities offer you a convenient scale of difficulty on which you can position yourself according to your capabilities. A good example would be birdwatching, which

can involve sitting watchfully in an easily accessible hide or trekking with a backpack over difficult terrain. Meditation, on the other hand, is easy in physical terms (unless you decide to force yourself into the lotus position) but offers the opportunity to explore profound realities, and a route towards peace of mind.

YOU AND YOURS
RETIREMENT AND THE FAMILY

Family connections are important, even when they're far from perfect. Retirement gives you the chance to bond closer with your partner, contribute to family life, and enjoy grandparenthood.

When you retire, you face expectations from others, and some of these will relate to the amount of time you have available – to socialize with them, to support them, and to take on some of their burdens. This, of course, is particularly an issue within the family, or in an unmarried partnership. Other issues may result from increased proximity between people used to spending more time apart.

Fresh partnerships
The greatest influence retirement has on relationships is its impact on the couple. Whether one partner is retired already or continues working, a process of adjustment, and sometimes even tension, can be expected. Two partners adjusting to retirement together can be an experience of either mutual support or exacerbated stress, depending

27%
TRICKY TRANSITIONS?
In an Australian Institute of Family Studies survey of adults aged 50–70, of those who had a partner who was retired, 27 per cent of women and 21 per cent of men **had trouble adjusting** to the new dynamic within the relationship when their spouse left work.

LIVE AND LET LIVE

People used to the hierarchy and control structures of a workplace may miss those reassuring features when they retire, and try to recreate them within the family. It's important for newly retired people to look out for such patterns of thought and behaviour within themselves, and take corrective measures, if necessary. The following watchpoints can help you avoid some of the pitfalls:

INVESTIGATE...
...any points of tension, so that you understand how they've arisen.

COMMUNICATE...
...regularly and openly with the members of your household, particularly about your changing feelings during retirement.

LISTEN...
...to the people you share your life with and look out for any unspoken implications. Be empathetic. Ask people how they feel about any lifestyle changes within the home.

PURSUE...
...your own interests actively, instead of simply tagging along with what your partner or other household members are doing.

on the individuals and their circumstances. Any time lag in retirement dates can create a completely new domestic set-up once the later retiree starts spending more time at home.

Retirement is also an opportunity for a couple to rediscover each other through shared activities, closer intimacy, and "parallel play" – simply being near each other while pursuing separate activities (see p163).

Generation game

The chance to refocus on family, and especially grandchildren, is one of the acknowledged positives of retirement. In the UK, a 1998 British Social Attitudes (BSA) survey revealed that 30 per cent of grandparents said they saw grandchildren several times a week. The relationship is usually quite close and satisfying, and is regarded as positive and important by both generations. Becoming a grandparent is a meaningful transition that often leads to a greater appreciation of your life experience, and a feeling of having moved into the next phase of life. Passing on wisdom to the next generation – as well as relishing their joyful and energetic company – can play a large part in your sense of contentment after retirement.

GRANDPARENT'S CHARTER

New to grandparenting? Here are some hints and tips to get you started:

- Get to know the other grandparents. Understanding the complete family dynamic can help you be more empathetic.
- Don't be offended if you're kept at a distance at times. Your son or daughter will need space to make their own parenting choices.
- Don't impose your own views – listen and defer to the parents.
- Volunteer practical help on a regular basis.
- Don't expect instant bonding with a new baby – let it happen in its own time.

CHAPTER 2

RIPE AND READY

PLANNING FOR RETIREMENT

LOOKING AHEAD
PLANNING AND IMPROVISING

Would you consider yourself to be a planner, on the whole, or do you prefer to do things on the fly? Most of us know that at least some forethought is better before retirement – so why do we differ so much?

When it comes to feeling positive about retirement, some kinds of planning are better than others. A 2012 study in Hong Kong met with volunteers both before and after they'd retired, and studied the effects of their plans. The researchers classified their plans into four sub-groups:

- Financial (eg savings and property ownership).
- Health (eg exercise and check-ups).
- Social (eg developing supportive networks through friendship groups or hobbies).
- Psychological (thinking about how to adapt to changes).

The researchers found that, while financial and health planning was simply sensible, social and psychological planning had conflicting effects. Having a detailed social plan made it harder to adjust to retirement – largely because it meant taking on new projects too quickly. Planning how to adapt psychologically, on the other hand, led to happier retirees. This doesn't mean that you shouldn't plan activities, of course, but that it might be wise to ease yourself into something new rather than jump straight in.

Living for the day?
Does retirement planning require a solemn attitude? Apparently not: according to a 2015 study published in *Work, Aging and*

HOW DO YOU VIEW TIME?

An Australian study placed people's attitude to time into five groups (shown below). Your tendency towards planning or improvising can depend on which group is most relevant to you. The study notes that a healthy mind actually has a reasonable balance of all of these elements.

1) Past positive: you feel warm and nostalgic when thinking about the past.
2) Past negative: bad memories have a strong hold on you.

3) Present fatalistic: you're focused on the here-and-now, but don't feel that your actions have much effect on things.
4) Present hedonistic: you're interested in instant gratification and don't think much about consequences.

5) Future oriented: you mostly think in terms of what's going to happen next, basing your thoughts on imagined future consequences of various courses of action.

⃝ MAKING PLANS: THE BIG FOUR

According to a theory set out by organizational psychologist Gary Adams, you should ask yourself:

1 **What will I do?** Think about how you'd like to fill your days – for example with domestic life, leisure pursuits, friends, or personal projects.

2 **How will I afford it?** Plot out how much money you'll need, where the funds will come from, and any sacrifices you're willing to make.

3 **Where will I live?** Perhaps you want to downsize an empty nest or free up some equity? Do you love your local area or fancy a change of scene?

4 **Who will I share it with?** Perhaps one of your children needs you more than the others. Are there old friends you'd like to spend more time with?

Retirement, good-time folks are among the stronger planners. Perhaps surprisingly, "present hedonistic" people (see above) were more likely to plan for retirement than those whose thoughts were either mainly in the past or mainly in the future. Enjoying life today, it was argued, motivated them to plan how to keep it enjoyable tomorrow.

Do I need to be a planner?
As you contemplate retirement, both the past and the future will be prominent in your mind – and it's very difficult to change your attitude towards them. A better approach might be to acknowledge that both planners and improvisers can learn from each other. If you're an improviser, try to be flexible:

look into financial and lifestyle arrangements that will give you the freedom to change your mind – for example, avoid tying up your funds in a single venture. If you're a planner, remember that a little adaptability is prudent: if your plans turn out disappointing, do you have a fallback? The studies point to including a bit of both: have a plan, but plan to adjust.

ROADMAP TO RETIREMENT
CHARTING YOUR LIFE

As you approach retirement, it's time to ask yourself some questions. Who are you now? What have been the major turns in your life? And what turns do you want to make past the next big transition?

When lifespans were shorter, retirement was a simpler proposition: it lasted a few years, and you used those years to rest and relax. Now that medical science has added years – even decades – to our life expectancies, retirement isn't just seen as a quiet sunset but a whole new phase of life. How does that affect our retirement decisions?

When do I stop work?
A US study released in 2014 found that people who expected to live a long life tended to defer their retirement. Specifically, those who thought that making it to 75 or 85 seemed likely were planning to delay their retirement by, on average, five months. Of course, one's actual lifespan can be hard to predict: health, habits, and family history all play a part; nothing's

MAKING A LIFE CHART
Which memories will be the best guide for your future in retirement? Try plotting out your major life events like this. List your accomplishments and any obstacles in chronological order, and rate each life experience for "pleasure" and "mastery" on a scale of 1–10, where 1 is the lowest and 10 is the highest. Finally, analyse your pleasure and mastery scores to identify the types of things that play to your strengths. You can then aim to incorporate as many "high-scoring" activities into your retirement as possible.

MY 20s:
I worked in low-level jobs after college
Pleasure: 2/10 – it was pretty boring.
Mastery: 4/10 – at least I was independent and supporting myself.

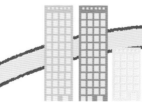

I scraped by and was living with friends
Pleasure: 8/10 – I liked the company.
Mastery: 2/10 – it was fairly relaxing.

MY 30s:
I was on my way up the career ladder
Pleasure: 6/10 – it made me feel good about myself. I enjoyed the PR and meeting new people.
Mastery: 7/10 – I felt competent managing teams and meeting deadlines.

I was married, with a young family
Pleasure: 9/10 – the kids were adorable and my marriage was good. I spent a lot of time with the family in parks and loved the outdoors.
Mastery: started 1/10, rose to maybe 6/10 – parenting was a steep learning curve!

certain in this world. Prioritizing emotional fulfilment seems like a good idea: that way, you can plan to be happy for as long as it lasts.

Pleasure and mastery

Try thinking of your life as a series of twists and turns, and examine which turns led you towards fulfilment and which led you away. To do this, you could adopt a technique used in cognitive behavioural therapy (CBT) by measuring your life experiences on two scales: "pleasure" and "mastery". The pleasure scale simply involves quantifying how much enjoyment you got out of something. The mastery scale measures how competent you felt – did getting on top of a difficult task, for example, give you a sense of satisfaction and give your confidence a boost? Psychologically speaking we need a healthy mix of both – pleasure

isn't that rewarding if it isn't backed up by a feeling of being in control and able to cope.

As you approach retirement, you will be dealing with more and more situations that challenge your sense of mastery. Most obviously, you'll be leaving your job, which may well have been your major source of it; dealing with diminished physical capacity could be another factor.

Visualizing the "road"

When thinking of your life as a journey, then, try imagining pleasure and mastery as different aspects of the road. Picture pleasure as the physical environment: was the road bumpy or smooth? Were you, figuratively speaking, driving in beautiful surroundings or in a wasteland; cruising along or fighting against the wind? Picture mastery, on the other hand, as the level of the

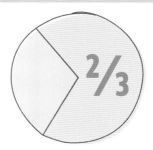

SENIOR SOCIETY
Two-thirds of the people who have lived **past the age of 65** in the entire history of the world **are alive right now**.

land. Were you in a "happy valley" feeling confident, or were you clinging to a high peak and suffering from vertigo? Now consider the turns that brought you to the calm valleys in your life. What did they have in common? As you think about your ideas for the future, what kind of road do they seem to take you along?

MY 40s:
The company folded and I had to go freelance
Pleasure: 5/10 – it was exciting when I did well, but the lack of security was stressful. I had more free time and spent it hiking.
Mastery: it ended up at about 8/10 once I got on top of things; I'm proud of myself for surviving.

I felt like the odd one out because my friends were all employed
Pleasure: 3/10 – a couple of them were very supportive, which meant a lot. I felt let down by others.
Mastery: 2/10 – I hated feeling like the only person not succeeding!

MY 50s:
I started running my own small company
Pleasure: 6/10 – it was nice being my own boss, but I had less time for family and friends than I wanted.
Mastery: 9/10 – everyone looked to me; I had to have the answers.

My daughter was having problems and getting into trouble
Pleasure: 1/10 – I felt miserable because I was worrying about her.
Mastery: 7/10 – I felt awful when I couldn't help her, but still managed to do some good.

MY 60s:
I'm thinking about selling the company
Pleasure: 4/10 – I feel like I've learned about as much as I'm going to from this experience.
Mastery: 5/10 – I feel on top of it, but not challenged. I'm daunted by the prospect of letting it go.

I wish I had more time with my family
Pleasure: 7/10 – I love them, but worry how we'll get along when I'm retired and around more.
Mastery: 3/10 – it could be a challenge!

I wish I could improve my social life
Pleasure: 6/10 – when I actually get to socialize.
Mastery: 2/10 – I haven't made any new friends for ages and worry that I've lost the knack.

FIT FOR THE FUTURE
STAYING HEALTHY

It can be hard to find time for exercise when you're still busy at work, but we all know that staying fit can extend and improve our lives. It can also put you in a strong position to tackle the challenges ahead.

Retirement can be a shock to the system. For one thing, unless you have substantial savings it's likely to mean a reduction in your income, which can lead to a phenomena known as the "income effect", whereby people with lower incomes are, empirically, more vulnerable to ill health.

If you're already in reasonable health, further developing your fitness levels can be a good cushion against potential stresses. It is also possible to maintain a degree of fitness even if you do have some health problems. Pyschologically, the sense of accomplishment experienced after exercise, especially if you've been doubting your abilities, can be a boost to your self-esteem.

Put simply, if you're feeling fit and well when you retire, you'll be in a much better position to be able to deal with any problems the transition throws at you.

Too late to get fit?
Undeniably, it takes energy to get into and maintain an exercise programme. If you're not in the first flush of youth, getting fit while you continue to work can seem like too much to handle — you may simply feel that you're due a rest. If you're retiring because your health is already a bit shaky then you may not be in the best condition to hit the gym — your doctor is your best guide here. You may prefer gentler methods — such as swimming or a brisk walk — but with a good

fitness instructor and perhaps a consultation with your doctor about any existing medical conditions, you might decide that you're ready for a challenge. For example, New York sports-medicine physician Jordan Metzl remarks that people over 60 "shouldn't be intimidated to do strength training. It really helps strengthen your muscles and

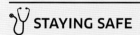
STAYING SAFE

If you try to do too much physical exercise too soon there's a chance you could injure yourself. (The same is true of everyone, no matter what their age.) If you're planning to start a fitness regime, seek medical advice first to make sure you're doing what's right for you. Don't be disheartened – even a seemingly unambitious regime can be great for your health and spirits. Remember the popular saying in the fitness community: "No matter how slow you go, you're still lapping the people on the couch."

GETTING YOUR HEART PUMPING

During exercise your heart rate (expressed as beats per minute, or bpm) speeds up – but by how much does it need to increase for you to get the most out of your exercise without overworking your heart? The American Heart Association recommends the following target heart rates (assuming you don't have a heart condition, in which case talk to your doctor). The ideal range is between 50–85 per cent of the average maximum rate for your age.

Age	Target heart rate during exercise (bpm)	Average maximum heart rate during exercise (bpm)
40 years	90–153	180
45 years	88–149	175
50 years	85–145	170
55 years	83–140	165
60 years	80–136	160
65 years	78–132	155
70 years	75–128	150

bones and reduces the risk of falling." If you start slow and build up, you might surprise yourself.

Spotting the opportunities

If your job comes with any fitness benefits, such as a company gym or an employee discount at a local leisure centre, not only might you want to take advantage of them now, you might also think about including them in your retirement negotiations (see pp78–81). Could you get your company to allow you to use its gym for a wind-down period, for example, or to extend your employee discount for the rest of the tax year?

Does your job naturally involve exercise? Do you have a long walk there and back, for example? Are there lots of stairs to climb? Do you pound a daily beat? You might want to make a note of how much exercise you're already doing (a pedometer is useful here): that way, you can anticipate what to compensate for once you retire so you don't find yourself losing fitness without realizing why.

(see pp78–81)

START THE CLOCK

Official **guidelines in both the UK and US** recommend that most healthy adults should aim to do at least...

2.5 hours

...of **moderate activity** each week (eg cycling or brisk walking), or...

1.25 hours

...of **vigorous, raise-a-sweat exercise** (eg running or a game of singles tennis). This can be done in bouts as short as...

10 minutes

Each week, you should also do some **muscle-strengthening activities** (eg press-ups or digging in the garden) on at least...

2 days

BRAIN GAMES

KEEPING YOUR MIND IN TRIM

If you've heard the expression "use it or lose it", you'll know how important it is to keep your wits sharp – especially as retirement nears. What you may not know is how much depends on your job.

While we might assume that someone whose job involves wrestling complex concepts is more likely to stay alert after retirement than someone with a routine role, the science suggests the opposite. A 2009 cross-cultural study held in the US and Sweden found that, while people with complex jobs tended to perform well on tests for things like verbal and spatial memory before they retired, once they did, they suffered more "cognitive decline". This may be because they had more to lose, but it seems that mental challenge at work doesn't necessarily protect you after you retire.

The exact reason for this is not fully understood, but the general view is that mental activity, like physical activity, is something that you have to keep doing if you want to stay good at it. The drop from daily challenge to quiet retirement might be hard on your brain.

How does my brain work?

What do we mean by mental activity anyway? The basic answer is that it's any brain-based skill you use to carry out a task. Like our bodies, our brains can start to go downhill as we age, and, while it's uncomfortable to acknowledge, this isn't entirely under our own control.

It's common to lose at least a bit of mental function in later life, so if you keep losing your keys, it probably means nothing – but

Q WHAT DOES MY BRAIN NEED TO DO?

These are the basic brain functions that make up your cognitive ability. Pre-retirement is a good time to check that you're still comfortable with what your brain can do. Search for tests and puzzles online using any of the terms below plus the words "puzzle" or "brain teaser".

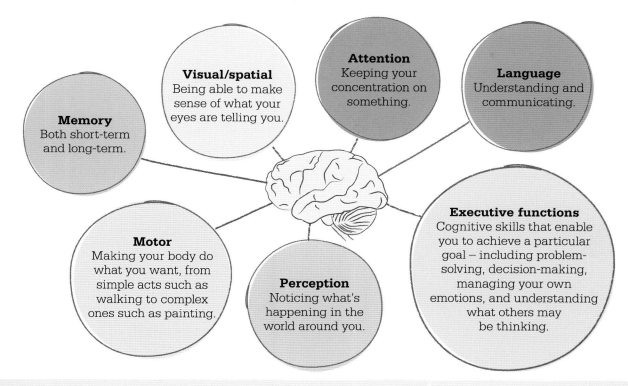

Visual/spatial
Being able to make sense of what your eyes are telling you.

Attention
Keeping your concentration on something.

Language
Understanding and communicating.

Memory
Both short-term and long-term.

Motor
Making your body do what you want, from simple acts such as walking to complex ones such as painting.

Perception
Noticing what's happening in the world around you.

Executive functions
Cognitive skills that enable you to achieve a particular goal – including problem-solving, decision-making, managing your own emotions, and understanding what others may be thinking.

there are some risk factors to watch out for. Studies suggest that cognitive decline is associated with things that you can easily check with your doctor, including: poor diet, chronic inflammation, diabetes, obesity, hormonal imbalance, hypertension, stress, and depression. So if you're planning to retire soon, it's a good idea to book an appointment. That way, you can either start tackling problems in advance or plan for potential difficulties.

WHAT SHOULD I EXPECT?

A certain amount of cognitive decline is normal as we age, but some skills usually last longer than others. If you have any worries about the areas mentioned below, the sooner (and younger) you address them the better.

Almost everyone loses a bit of...	You might want to see your doctor if you're losing...
■ Memory	■ Vocabulary
■ Mental processing speed	■ Numerical skills
■ Ability to multitask	■ General knowledge
■ High-level reasoning	■ Ability to perform simple tasks
■ Executive function (see above)	■ Sense of direction in familiar places

EYE ON THE CALENDAR
GETTING THE TIMING RIGHT

You know you want to go – but exactly when and how? Getting the timing right can be crucial, so if retirement is starting to look tempting, what questions should you be asking yourself?

The time of year you choose to retire can be surprisingly important. Whether you decide to leave in summer or winter, for example, might depend on whether you feel more confident about your physical or psychological health. You'll want to feel like your retirement is a happy time, so think about what will seem cheerful as well as sensible. Also, if you're in a relationship, discuss both the practical details and emotional effects before you make a decision: whether you intend to retire together or at different times can have an affect on how you experience retirement.

ⓘ SHOULD I LEAVE IN SUMMER?

- Most of us find it easier to picture a "new beginning" when the weather is warm.

- The quality of light can also affect our mental health: seasonal affective disorder (SAD) is a form of clinical depression that's strongly associated with the shorter, darker days of winter. Since there's some evidence that retirees are more vulnerable to depression anyway, you might prefer to take the step in a brighter season.

(?) SHOULD I LEAVE IN WINTER?

- If your physical health is your main concern – or if you're just feeling a bit tired and worn out – this could be the perfect time to retire. Taking it easy might be a better prospect than heading off to work in the cold.

- The older you get, the more at risk you are from common winter bugs. Certainly, doctors are more insistent about things like flu jabs for the over-65s. So a train or office full of sniffling commuters and co-workers may not be very appealing.

(?) SHOULD ONE OF US STAY ON?

- If one partner stays on at work while the other retires, you're likely to have more money flowing into the household.

- Although it might be harder for the "pioneer" retiree – they'll be at home on their own, testing the waters – the second retiree can learn from their experience.

- There is a chance that the retired one will find themselves in need of more emotional support – which might put extra pressure on the one still going off to work every day.

(?) SHOULD WE LEAVE TOGETHER?

- Synchronizing your work end dates means you can be there for each other as you adjust to retirement. However, if you both suffer from culture shock, you'll have to work it out together rather than compete over who's the "upset one".

- If one of you was always more the "worker" (whether practically or psychologically), they may be dealing with a bigger identity adjustment than a partner who always had one foot in the home-maker role.

READY TO FIRE THE STARTING PISTOL?

As well as taking into account the time of year and your partner's plans, expert Jim Yih identifies five common "triggers" to retirement:

1	**EMPLOYER**	The company is downsizing and has offered a good incentive package.
2	**TIME / TENURE**	You've "done" your 30 or 35 years and earned your pension credits.
3	**CHANGE**	You're just bored and want to do something different.
4	**MONEY**	You've got enough money and feel no need to earn any more.
5	**PLAN**	You've got a plan, and have met the conditions you intended to meet.

RETIREMENT IS NOT AN EVENT BUT A PROCESS AND ONE THAT SHOULD BEGIN LONG BEFORE YOU TURN IN YOUR RETIREMENT PAPERS

JERRY CHASEN
ATTORNEY AND LIFE COACH

BUILDING A NEST EGG
THE PSYCHOLOGY OF MONEY

Are we good at handling money? For many of us, the answer may be "not really". But is this just a personality trait, or are circumstances beyond our control making it harder for us to plan ahead?

When you think about financial planning for your retirement, how do you feel? Do you feel a sense of excitement, as if you're preparing for a treat or an adventure? Perhaps you feel sensible and calm? Or do you have a sinking feeling in the pit of your stomach, dreading a closer study of something you're sure will be bad news? Some of us are more comfortable planning than others as a matter of disposition, of course, but the science suggests that outside forces play a big role.

What's discouraging you?
According to a 2013 study by economists Eric Brucker and Karen Leppel in the US, the biggest obstacles to planning were procrastination, inertia, and low expectations of success. Not surprisingly these were found to be more common among the poorer workers they studied. If you've got plenty of money – rich people were among the biggest planners, they found – then thinking about what you'll do with it is a much nicer experience than thinking about how you might manage without it if you're nearly broke.

Men versus women
The same study found that when it came to retirement planning, there were more men than women in the high-planning group. Are men just more sensible than women? Actually it's more about social roles; to quote a 2005 study by sociologists Phyllis Moen, Stephen Sweet, and Raymond Swisher: while planning tended to "operate similarly for both men and women in similar circumstances, men and women are seldom in similar circumstances." Women were more likely to base their career plans around their spouses', more likely to expect to retire early, and less likely to have a solid amount of money to retire on. Historically, women have had less money and less control over their

> After a person's basic needs have been met... the relationship between **income and happiness** is quite small.
>
> **Ryan T. Howell**
> Professor of Psychology at San Francisco State University

careers than men. Women also tend to have more disjointed careers (taking time out to have children, for example), making it harder to build up a nest egg.

How to beat the block

If you don't happen to be wealthy, how do you tackle the mental block? Both studies propose gaining a greater sense of control.

Moen, Sweet, and Swisher noted that our social networks have a strong influence on how confident we feel about planning. Watching what co-workers do, and the informal discussions we have when we get home, are important it seems. If we're given incentives and structures – such as the 401(k) plan in the US – we tend to do better, too. Brucker and Leppel, meanwhile, wrote optimistically of improving people's access both to education and financial planners; "fun, game-like software" was on their wish list.

In the absence of retirement-planning computer games, what can you do? The best advice seems to be to expose yourself to planning in a way that doesn't feel too daunting. Brucker and Leppel noted that people who've spoken to a financial planner tended to be well prepared; this may not just be because they got good advice, but because the act of speaking to a planner in itself gets you thinking about it.

Making things fun is also good advice. Who do you know who's a good planner and also good company? Are there places you like to go – such as a local café or library – that could become "planning zones"? We're supposed to be sober and serious about financial planning, but making things feel rewarding is often the best way of getting them done.

WHO ARE THE BIGGEST FINANCIAL PLANNERS?

In 2013, **economists Eric Brucker** and **Karen Leppel** found that the biggest planners tended to be:

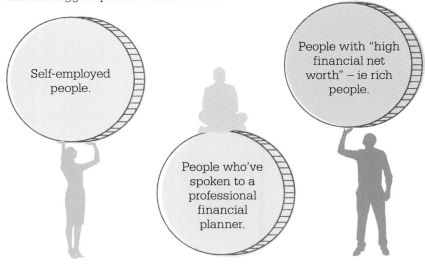

Self-employed people.

People who've spoken to a professional financial planner.

People with "high financial net worth" – ie rich people.

What's the **common factor?** All of these people have either experience or support in **managing their money**. If you feel you lack both, support may be the first thing to seek.

75%

PIGGY BANK RAID

In the US, the 401(k) defined-contribution pension has largely replaced corporate pensions, but self-management isn't always a long-term benefit – **75 per cent of older people** borrow from their 401(k) plans before retirement to cover other expenses.

TIME TO QUIT?

THE EARLY RETIREMENT OPTION

Feeling your age? Responsibilities to meet? Or do you want to enjoy your vitality while it lasts? If you have plans for the future and can negotiate it to your advantage, early retirement might be for you.

According to the *European Journal of Public Heath*, there are three main reasons for retiring early:

- Ill health – you may just not feel up to working.
- Financial reasons – you've been offered a good package or the timing works well for you.
- The job isn't rewarding – you may want out of a dull and repetitive or demanding and stressful job.

Of course, you might simply feel that you'd like to retire so you can enjoy your health while it lasts. Taking early retirement doesn't necessarily mean stopping work either: you might want to seize a new opportunity.

How do I go about it?

Some employers are happy to accept early retirement, or even offer it as an incentive if they're trying to cut down their workforce. However, if your employer isn't so keen, what are your options?

26.7%

ON THE MONEY

The British civil service is known for its **solid pension schemes**, and it seems to show; a study conducted in 2000 found that out of 2,532 civil servants, **26.7 per cent retired early** when they had the chance.

IN THE CULTURE – WHEN DO WE RETIRE?

The official retirement age varies from country to country but, according to a 2012 international study, we often retire much earlier. In general, women tend to retire one or two years earlier than men.

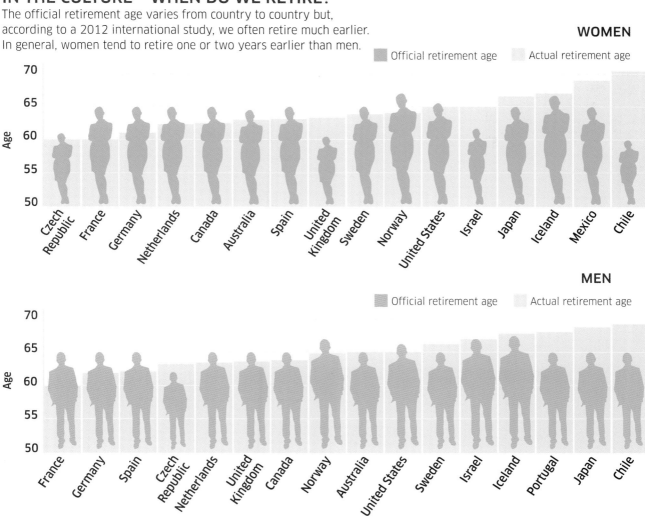

WOMEN

Official retirement age   Actual retirement age

MEN

Official retirement age   Actual retirement age

A lot can depend on the culture: some companies see it as disloyalty and put up resistance, while others are more flexible. If early retirement is your idea rather than your employer's, how will it affect any pensions or settlements? How much can you persuade them it's in their interests to let you go? Could you negotiate a phased retirement (see pp82–83) instead?

How will it affect me?
You'll also want to consider the psychological effects. At least one study, carried out in 2010 at the University of Michigan, found that retiring in your early 60s can make you more vulnerable to cognitive decline (see pp62–63), so if you're looking at a sharp drop-off in terms of intellectual stimulation and social support –

for example, your job is your main brainwork and most of your friends are colleagues – then try to arrange retirement activities that keep you challenged.

The best advice is to look before you leap. If you can afford it and you've got something better to move on to, early retirement might turn out to be the start of a whole new life.

STAYING ON

THE LATE RETIREMENT OPTION

If your job is still interesting, or you want more time to build up your savings, you might want to stay at work for a little while longer. What are your options, and how will late retirement affect your state of mind?

Whether a late retirement is for you may depend on what your job demands of you physically. If most of your day is spent at a desk, you're likely to have more freedom to choose than if you work in a job that requires physical strength and stamina. After a certain point, you may need to try and move into a more supervisory role or scale back on the heaviest work.

Is it in the culture?

A lot also hangs on the society you live in: is it one that values older workers? While we'd all like to believe our fate is entirely in our own hands, we're also all limited by what our society allows. Some cultures, for example, view "elders" as teachers (which may or may not be a role that appeals to you), while others favour the energy of youth. The key to navigating these different roles may be to demonstrate creativity. A 2008 study in the *Graziadio Business Review* found that most cultures tended to see older people as less imaginative and

> Employment **options** for older workers **continue to evolve**.
>
> **Donald M. Atwater, PhD and Daniela Pop**
> *Graziadio Business Review*

more set in their ways, so to be seen as valuable, the best idea is not just to come up with inventive ideas and solutions, but to make sure people notice how inventive you've been.

Is it right for me?

Dr Elizabeth Mokyr Horner in California found that, no matter what age we retire, we all tend to go through the same psychological stages of adjustment: an initial spike in wellbeing, followed by a rapid fall in happiness levels a few years later, and then a stabilizing of happiness levels in the long run. So go with what feels right for you and retire in your own time.

✎ ARE YOU PSYCHOLOGICALLY READY FOR RETIREMENT?

Try this quiz to find out if you're ready to retire, or if staying on might make you happier:

1 How important is your job when it comes to getting a sense of life satisfaction?

A Very important: my job is central to my identity.
B Fairly important: I like feeling useful.
C It's something to do, but it's not the be-all and end-all.
D Not much at all, really.

2 How many non-work activities do you have that give you a sense of purpose?

A Not very many, really.
B I have some hobbies or interests, but they've always been secondary to work.
C I've got a fair amount going on.
D I've got things going on that I love, and I wish I could spend more time on them.

3 How do you imagine your life will be once you stop working?

A I find it hard to picture, and rather an uncomfortable idea.
B A break would be nice, but I don't have many plans.
C I've got some ideas I'd like to explore.
D I've got very definite plans.

4 How do you think retirement will affect your relationship with your family and friends?

A I've usually been too busy to spend much time with them – it'll be a new experience.
B I haven't thought about it.
C We'll have to re-adjust, but hopefully we'll work it out.
D We've talked about it, and we'll tackle the changes of retirement together.

5 How much energy for work do you have these days?

A Bring it on, I can take it.
B I'm not going to wear myself out, but I feel OK.
C I'm losing steam a little.
D I'm pretty close to having had enough.

Answers:

Mostly As: You're probably not ready to retire yet but you should still put some thought into it: going from a job you're deeply invested in to retirement can be a big culture shock.

Mostly Bs: Late retirement sounds like a good option as you're so comfortable in your job. Retirement, when it comes, will be a change, and you'll probably want to line up new tasks and goals.

Mostly Cs: Emotionally, you're ready for retirement. If you do stay in your job, however, it's likely to be for financial reasons, and you may find work a strain. If so, get plenty of support while you're still working and talk to a financial adviser about making retirement possible.

Mostly Ds: It sounds like your heart is already out of the door! Retirement is your next big project and your job is just marking time until you can move on. If you can afford to go, an early retirement might well be for you.

PRESSURE TO GO
THE INVOLUNTARY RETIREMENT

What if you want to stay on but find that you can't? We'd all like to wrap up our careers on our own terms, but sometimes circumstances get the better of us. How do you manage then?

Before the 1970s and 80s, there wasn't much choice about retirement: you either stopped work for health reasons or you reached the official age and that was the end of your career. Since then, however, many countries have abolished the legal retirement age. It's supposed to be your choice when to go – but that's not always how it happens.

An uncomfortable exit

Nobody likes to feel they have no control over the important parts of their life, and being pressured to retire is upsetting. Retirees who view their retirement as voluntary have been found, according to a study published in the *Journal of Vocational Behaviour*, to rate their life satisfaction higher and to feel both mentally and physically healthier than those who feel it wasn't their choice.

Feeling forced out?

The pressure might be subtle – comments, disrespect, either loading you with more work than anyone could manage or sending you so little that you feel bored and useless. There's also the major issue of "redundancy". The company might be genuinely downsizing – but if it's always at the expense of older employees, this could be age discrimination.

If that's happening to you, research your legal position. Most nations have laws that call for equal treatment regardless of age, and there are organizations that can advise you on your rights.

You may need to advocate for yourself, either to stay on at work or press for a better leaving package: whatever you decide to do, knowing your rights is the first step.

If you do lose out, you may have to do some psychological adjustment. It's only natural to be unhappy at ending your career on an involuntary note, but it doesn't invalidate your life's work and it doesn't make you a failure. If circumstances do get the better

20-30%

WHO DECIDES?

Studies consistently indicate that **20–30 per cent of retirees** feel retirement **wasn't their decision**, and statistics from the International Social Survey Programme suggest the figure in **Western countries** may be as high as **50 per cent**.

✎ KEEPING RECORDS

If employers and colleagues are making you feel unwelcome without explicitly telling you to go, and you're planning to challenge that, your first step is to keep detailed records. Don't keep them somewhere that could be accessed by hostile people – such as a company computer – but if something happens, make a note of everything that was said, including the date, time, and any witnesses. If you're going to make a case you'll need evidence, and the more concrete it is, the better.

of you, be aware that this puts you at a greater risk of depression, anxiety, and other stress-related illnesses. Be proactive and make sure you get support in advance.

Staying positive

Being unable to manage the basic circumstances of your life is frustrating, and if you're feeling pressured to retire, you're probably pretty tense right now. Don't let the tension stop you from thinking about retirement activity plans, however. It may feel like giving in, and you may stay to fight another day, but you will probably retire eventually, and when you do, you'll want activity and meaning in your life. Feeling confident that that activity and meaning will be there – even if you don't want it there yet – may help you negotiate for yourself from a position of emotional strength.

? WHAT'S MAKING YOU GO?

Common reasons for involuntary retirement can come from either your personal life or from work. Each of these reasons can be painful, but they may need different coping mechanisms: being disempowered from above means dealing with frustration and possibly humiliation, while personal circumstances mean coming to terms with a potentially permanent life change.

COMMON PERSONAL REASONS

Declining health and strength
- Stay positive about your capabilities, and invest more time in doing the things you're still good at.
- Avoid becoming overly focused on your health.
- Be grateful for the health you do have and the care you're receiving.

Needing to support an unwell spouse
- Get as much help and support as possible.
- Feel the positive impact of easing the suffering of someone close to you.
- Make sure you're caring for yourself as well as for someone else.

COMMON WORK-BASED REASONS

Unpleasant working environment
- Don't blame yourself for others' attitudes; remember that you can only control your own actions and reactions.
- Focus on the lessons you've learned from dealing with a toxic situation.
- Embrace your newfound freedom!

Redundancy or dismissal
- Try not to take it personally – you're not responsible for economic cycles or company restructuring.
- Keep active and positive – don't wallow in dejection.
- Talk with friends and loved ones; sharing the load will go a long way towards minimizing stress.

KNOWING YOUR STRENGTHS
A PERSONAL STOCKTAKE

Forget money and practical concerns for a moment, and ask yourself this: what actually makes you happy? What are the ways you really enjoy life? What positive habits can you take with you into retirement?

Psychology has traditionally focused on our neuroses and damage. This makes a certain amount of sense: the people most likely to seek out a psychologist are unhappy people, and if someone comes to a psychologist saying they're unhappy, the natural question is: "Why?" However, there's a more recent movement – positive psychology – that argues we can learn at least as much by focusing on people's talents and virtues. When it comes to retirement, there's a lot to be said for that.

Figuring it out

There's a useful acronym in positive psychology, which refers to the five elements of wellbeing: PERMA (see opposite). By addressing each element in turn you can do a stocktake of your own happiness skills, which will put you in a strong position to tackle the challenges ahead. According to positive psychology pioneer Martin Seligman, optimism is a habit you can cultivate, and now, as you approach a major change, is a good time to get some practice.

> Greater ability to **savour positive experiences** [leads to] greater happiness, lower depression, and greater satisfaction.
>
> **Jennifer L. Smith and Linda Hollinger-Smith**
> *Aging & Mental Health*

"PERMA" – THE FIVE ELEMENTS OF WELLBEING

Element	Definition	How it applies to you in retirement
P **Positive Emotion**	A sustainable good mood that allows you to enjoy each day – or, on the difficult days, to find at least opportunities for pleasure that give you a sense of counterbalance and make the world feel like a good place.	As you approach retirement, look for ways to enjoy moments that aren't about work. A beautiful sunset, a good joke, a non-work task you feel proud of: these will all last beyond the job. We can practise our pleasure in life just like we'd exercise a muscle; the sooner you start, the better.
E **Engagement**	Also described as "flow", this is the ability to feel truly involved in your activities, which makes you feel competent, keeps your mind active and refreshed, and makes your life feel full and interesting.	If your job offered opportunities for engagement you shouldn't relinquish flow when you stop work. You might want to carry on into self employment or perhaps you have your eye on a hobby. Try thinking back to when you were younger – what did you engage in that made time fly by?
R **Positive Relationships**	Feeling part of a supportive community. This makes you feel loved and valuable; it also gives you the opportunity to love and value other people, which keeps your attitude towards humanity positive.	In retirement, the proportion of our relationships changes: less time with colleagues, more time with family. That might be a blessing, but it may also bring some strains. The best advice is to include as many positive relationships as possible rather than overloading the family circle.
M **Meaning**	A double benefit: both feeling good about yourself for being part of something that matters to you, and the freedom to think in terms of the broader picture and care about things beyond yourself. A job can be a convenient stand-in for that.	In the lead up to retirement, it's time to start thinking about what "bigger" thing really reflects your values. Any participation can give us a sense of meaning, but why not take the opportunity to be more selective now?
A **Accomplishment or Achievement**	We get a natural sense of pride when we feel we've bettered ourselves, mastered something, or achieved something difficult. We don't need to feel better than other people, but feeling competent and satisfied with ourselves is healthy.	Meeting challenges helps keep our minds young, and having a stock of new achievements means that our self-esteem stays robust and we experience retirement as a new phase of life rather than the end of something.

STRIKING A DEAL

NEGOTIATING YOUR EXIT

When you've done your job conscientiously, you deserve to leave with a good deal. How do you make sure you can arrange it – or cope with the frustration if that proves difficult?

While we'd all like to be millionaires, most of us just want a fair settlement. Depending on your employer, that can be a very straightforward or a very contentious business.

The unspoken contract

There's an interesting concept known as the "psychological contract", described by US psychologists Lynn McFarlane Shore and Lois E. Tetrick as "the employee's perception of the reciprocal obligations

? WHAT CAN YOU NEGOTIATE?

Don't limit your requests to just a pension, health plan, or golden handshake. Could you:

1 Take home an old office computer you've used for years?

2 Negotiate a mutually agreed-upon reference?

3 Agree to have first refusal on any freelance work for the next three years?

4 Retain access to company facilities such as a gym?

5 Accept some shares instead of a straightforward cash settlement?

6 Keep using a company car?

GETTING THE TIMING RIGHT

Bosses vary in their temperaments. Some people will automatically say no if they feel put on the spot, but might, for example, be more likely to say yes if you email them last thing on a Friday so they have a couple of days to think it over. Others might be ditherers who'll talk themselves out of generosity given too much time, but agree to more if you bargain face-to-face and then put it in writing straight away. Think of times when you've negotiated successfully in the past, then use the following steps to analyse why it worked:

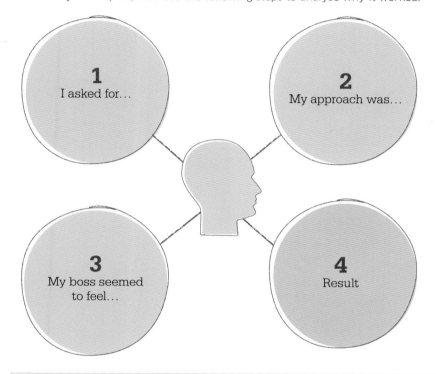

1 I asked for…

2 My approach was…

3 My boss seemed to feel…

4 Result

existing with their employer". In simple terms, if you work for someone, it's natural to feel that each of you owes the other certain considerations that may not have been explicitly stated, such as respect for each others' wishes and concern for each others' wellbeing. The tricky thing, as the psychologists note, is that the contract is "inherently subjective": because it's not explicit, it depends on your own perceptions – and an employer may have a different interpretation.

Types of obligation

Part of the problem is that working for people involves two different models of obligation – the "transactional" and the "relational". In a transactional exchange, it's straightforward: you perform certain services for an agreed economic reward – your salary or your pension. Negotiations are supposed to focus on the transactional (business is business, right?), but in fact there's usually also an element of the relational. The relational model feels more personal: a simple example would be the favour. You do a favour for someone, they owe you a favour back, or they at least owe you a degree of respect, fondness, or loyalty. If you've ever gone above and beyond for your employer, you probably have done them a favour of sorts – but if the employer sees that as merely transactional (you were doing your job, you got paid, end of story), then that can cause emotional strain. Communities run on relationships, and it upsets all of us when we feel that a relational obligation isn't repaid: we feel used and cheated, and it can permanently sour things between people.

Putting theory into action

You and your employer might have a cordial and cooperative relationship, in which case negotiating a good retirement deal might be quite straightforward. However,

>> employers aren't always that helpful, so you do need to press for your own interests.

If you're retiring by your own choice, the first thing to do is check your contract and see what it allows for. Your requests need to be realistic, and the more you can back them up with documentation, the better.

Relational obligations

If the documentation doesn't quite favour you, however, you needn't despair – if the company can be persuaded to be flexible, it might turn out to your advantage. Say, for example, there's a specific time limit that you don't quite meet – a better pension kicks in at age 65 and you're 63, or after 20 years service and you've been there for 18. Rather than seeing that as a closed door, consider it as something that might be in your reach if you stretch for it. If you've done anything extra for your employer, that might be the time to try and appeal to his or her sense of relational obligation; this won't work unless you know your boss well, but if there is anyone in authority who has a history of recognizing favours as well as a simple transaction, they may be the one to speak to.

It's not personal

Considering the psychological contract in this way can be helpful when it comes to getting

NEGOTIATING TACTICS

If you have to haggle a bit, what are the best ways to make your case? Try the following:

Present your requests one at a time. Presenting them all at once might overwhelm your employer and get an automatic refusal.

Lead with the request you think they're most likely to agree to. What psychologists call the "foot in the door phenomenon" can work to your advantage: people who've agreed to do something small for you are more likely to agree to something bigger later.

Focus on your value rather than your needs. You're terminating a business relationship, and employers pressed to feel concern about you once it ends may be resentful: stick to business rather than emotion.

your way. It's also useful in making things feel less personal: even if your employer isn't being good about negotiations, it can help you to feel less betrayed. Rather than harbouring the painful thought, "I guess all I did for them meant nothing!", it's a way of saying to yourself, "I guess they're doing this on the transactional model. Okay then: I don't owe them any favours either; let's just both get what we can out of this."

? NEED A "BRIDGE" TO RETIREMENT?

Suppose you need to work a little longer to maximize your leaving benefits but the company wants you to go now. The key in this situation is research and negotiation. For example: has the company offered any better deals to other employees that set a precedent? Were you ever reassured in the past, even verbally, that you wouldn't be made redundant? Could you move to a different position in the company temporarily? Has your employer said anything that could be seen as age discrimination? Armed with this information, you might want to seek legal advice, or just negotiate as cannily as you can.

? NEED HELP WITH THE PRESSURE?

Companies aren't always above using pressure. Employment attorney Alan L. Sklover notes, for example, that unfairly bad performance reviews can be used to create a feeling that you need to jump before you're pushed. Another tactic is the use of Human Resources (HR) to handle all the discussion: they don't have to work alongside you, so are often more comfortable refusing to budge. You don't have to accept that, however: as consultant Alan Johnson points out, "You probably don't work for HR, so talk to your boss about staying on a bit longer." It's harder to say no to someone who's worked for you for years, so use that to your advantage.

? NEED FURTHER SUPPORT?

Look around to see if you have any allies, whether they're stay-on employees or fellow unwilling retirees who might join you in negotiation. If you're friendly with anyone higher up in the organization, talk to them and make sure they let HR know that they're aware of your situation. You may, in the run of things, be a gentle and cooperative person, but this might be a time to play power politics.

Seeking advice

Meanwhile, consider whether you need legal advice. Severance attorney Jason Stern proposes asking for "time to review it with an attorney" before signing anything – even if you don't plan to appoint one, it shows you mean business. (After all, the company will doubtless have lawyers, so fair's fair.) This tactic may work better in some cultures and companies than others, but it's worth knowing in case you need it. Most of us aren't lawyers and may not be entirely comfortable with "playing hardball". Sometimes, however, you may just need to look at your retirement as a challenge to solve rather than as a quiet exit. After all, you don't stand to lose anything by trying – and you might gain a lot.

✎ PLAN OF ATTACK?

It can be helpful to draw up a plan for your optimum deal. List what you'd really like as regards:

- **Pension** – how much do you think is fair, and how do you want it to be paid?
- **Benefits** – what do you still want the company to cover after you no longer work there?
- **Ongoing business relationships** – do you want to keep working with the company in a freelance capacity?

- **Control over timing** – decide exactly when you want to leave and whether you might wind down to part-time work for a while.
- **Other specific perks** – for example, if your company sells products you might buy, could you keep your employee discount?

Once you've listed everything, rank them in order of priority. You might even include a few benefits you don't really care about, so that if you have to haggle, you have some requests that are easy to discard.

HALF IN, HALF OUT

THE PHASED RETIREMENT

Want to stop, but not quite yet? Nowadays, leaving work doesn't have to be an either-or: you could, instead, negotiate to retire at a more gradual rate, winding down rather than walking away.

You might be thinking about retiring, but would like a slower exit. Perhaps you still need the income but want to prioritize your health or spend more time with your grandchildren. The solution could be to scale back your hours and responsibilities over a period of months or years. This would allow you to continue your career while extending your free time.

What are the advantages?

There's evidence to suggest that a phased retirement may offer some protection against cognitive decline (see pp62–63), but does it necessarily make you happier? One major advantage is that it gives you a feeling of autonomy over your own life. If you want to retire slowly and your employers are supportive, the very fact of having your wishes respected is a positive thing.

Phased retirement has a practical advantage, too: it allows you to get used to the changes in your life and try out new activities without cutting yourself off from your old life. By keeping reliable and familiar activities in your life, it's easier to chalk off failed new projects or disappointing new hobbies to experience. In fact, it may free you up, psychologically, to try a variety of new activities until you find what works best.

Will the boss agree?

Deciding you'd prefer phased retirement is one thing; actually arranging it is another. Some companies are more cooperative than others – which may partly depend on their size (see top graph, opposite). Tax and labour laws can make it awkward for employers, too. However, it's worth knowing that even if a company doesn't have a formal policy for phased retirement they may still consider it: according to a 2007 study by the Center for Retirement Research at Boston College, nearly three times as many employers agreed to phased retirement as had a formal policy about it (see bottom graph, opposite).

Is it the right choice?

A lot may depend on how much you like your job – and whether you're making time for fun activities or for worrying duties, such as caring for a sick relative. (If you do have worries, however, it's still better to have time to deal with them.) Whatever you finally decide, having a sense of control is an unbeatable feeling.

EXPLORING YOUR OPTIONS

Q How cooperative will your employer be?

A It may depend on its size: bigger companies are more likely to have a formal phasing-out process. A 2005 US study found the following statistics:

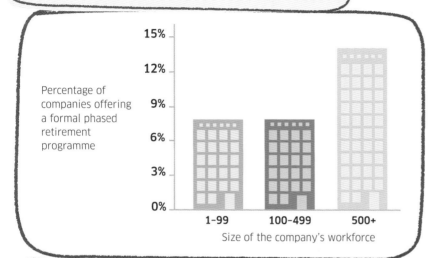

Percentage of companies offering a formal phased retirement programme

Size of the company's workforce

Q Do I need a formal structure?

A Possibly not: a study at Boston College found that companies were often willing to arrange phased retirement even if they didn't have a formal policy for it:

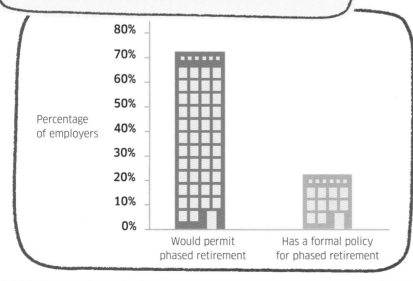

Percentage of employers

Would permit phased retirement

Has a formal policy for phased retirement

WHO'S IN?

A 2011 study in the US asked people over 50 if they'd be interested in **phased retirement**. Of those still in work...

38%

...said they would be interested.

46%

...of those interested said they'd like to **start the process** between the ages of **60 and 64**.

78%

...of those interested said it would **encourage** them to **work past** their **expected retirement age**.

MISSED OPPORTUNITY?

Of those who had **already retired**...

40%

...said they **would have been interested** in phased retirement **if it had been offered** to them.

33%

...said they **would have stayed in work longer** if they could have had a phased retirement.

WISDOM ON TAP

PREPARING FOR CONSULTANCIES

You've accumulated a lot of knowledge in the course of your working life. Now that you're ready to retire, is there a way to keep turning that knowledge to profitable account?

Wouldn't it be great to earn money simply by virtue of our experience and intelligence without having to do so much of the grind work? That's the consultancy dream: moving out of regular employment and instead becoming a called-in expert. How realistic is this as a plan?

GETTING STARTED

To set yourself up as a successful consultant you'll need several things:

- Demonstrable expertise in a subject on which people want to consult.

- A strong professional network to tap into for potential clients.

- To research the market for your talents. This could be advising companies (including your own if there's a skills gap while they find a replacement) or training new people.

- To research the competition. Be aware of balance here: if there are lots of people already doing it, does it mean there's a big market or that the market's saturated? If nobody's doing it, does it mean there's a gap to fill or that the market's not there? In short, is what you can offer something people will buy?

Q THE PSYCHOLOGY OF CONSULTING

As a form of semi-retirement, consulting can be a way to enjoy some of the satisfactions of full retirement while keeping one foot in the world of work. One of its advantages is to ease the psychological transition, and give you time to set up additional activities that will come into their own later, once you've left the workplace for good. Successful, highly driven people in particular, who may otherwise find the loss of job satisfaction in retirement a challenge, may relish the stimulation of staying in the thick of the action. Keeping intellectually fresh in this way can even help stave off cognitive decline.

✒ MAKING IT WORK

As an independent consultant you'll need to be your own marketeer. This means:

- Trading on contacts you've made while working. This should ideally begin before you start your retirement.

- Building an online presence. A solid-looking website is vital: if people can't get hold of you quickly they probably won't bother, and if they search for you and your site looks unprofessional they'll draw a negative inference about the quality of your work. Unless you're a website designer, you might want to bring in a professional to set it up.

- Building an offline presence. Get your face seen at seminars, trade fairs, and anywhere else you can hand out your card to potential clients.

✒ NEED A "PLAN B"?

If you'd prefer not to set up on your own, there are other options you could consider:

- Some staffing and recruitment firms are setting up specifically to place older consultants with clients seeking advice on their particular subject. At the moment, those subjects tend to be in marketing, healthcare, insurance, tourism, IT, and telecommunications. If those aren't your fields, it's worth doing your own research to see if there's a niche you fit.

- Your old company may be willing to re-hire you as a freelancer or part-timer – even if they were previously reluctant to offer a formal phased retirement (see pp82–83); tax and labour laws can make phasing-out a complicated proposition for employers.

GOT WHAT IT TAKES?
You may need to **hone your credentials**: consultants often require an **impressive resumé**; the recruiters YourEncore, for example, who have about...

9,000

...**consultants on their books**, look for people with an average of...

25 years'

...experience in their field. **In addition**, about...

60%

...of the consultants on their books have an **advanced degree**.

GOING SOLO

STARTING A RETIREMENT ENTERPRISE

After a lifetime of working for other people, the idea of being your own boss can be enormously appealing. If your inner entrepreneur is ready to come out, how do you go about going it alone?

Many of us would like to stay active – both financially and mentally – when we stop work. Starting your own business seems ideal: a way to make money and keep life interesting without giving up your independence. This may well be the case, but it's crucial both to assess your mental preparedness and put careful plans in place before you start.

A risky business?

You should take a clear-eyed look at how comfortable you are with risk. There's no point spending your entire retirement biting your nails to the quick: if you're one of nature's worriers, stick to something with limited start-up costs so you have less to worry about. If you decide it's not for you after all, then you might want to consider alternative ways of staying active and making ends meet, such as a phased retirement (see pp82–83).

It's also important to consider how your choice of business might affect your long-term happiness; it must be one you'll be content to work at over a long period of time. A 2002 study found that entrepreneurs over 50 were more likely to get "locked in" to their businesses even if they weren't happy there, simply because the employment opportunities elsewhere favour younger workers.

Crunching the numbers

Before you commit, draw up a strict financial plan. This is particularly important, both because of age discrimination and because you have fewer years to recoup any losses. As Nancy Collamer, author of *Second-Act Careers: 50+ Ways to Profit from Your Passions During Second Retirement*, puts it: "The general rule is: you shouldn't invest more than you can afford to lose." Retirement funds are best left as a safety net in case your enterprise falls through; run the numbers and make sure that you can still live with the worst-case scenario.

What do you do best?

It's often sensible to base your venture on something you already know how to do. The majority of successful retiree entrepreneurs use the knowledge and contacts they already have to build up their own niche business; a smaller section go professional with a hobby, such as woodworking or crafts. The one thing you probably shouldn't do is start a new venture with no experience at all: the odds of an unforeseen pitfall are just too high.

Building up your skills

There's a good chance that some areas in your skill set could do with improvement. Financial planning, bookkeeping, legal requirements, and taxes: these are the essential skills of running a business. Community college, business school, and adult education are your friend here: sign up for a course before you get started so you have the practical side covered. A solid grip on the basics is essential, and learning new skills is a great way to keep your brain active (see pp62–63).

Practical matters

You may also need to think about how your new venture will affect your living environment. If you're setting up as a dog-walker, for example, you might only need

23.6%

LATE START-UPS

In 2013, 23.6 per cent of new businesses in the US were started by **entrepreneurs aged 55 to 64**.

18–24 months

STAY CONNECTED

Don't let your contacts go stale. Martha Sargent, co-author of *Retire – and Start Your Own Business*, estimates that contacts, especially in high-tech industries, are "good for **about 18 to 24 months**".

a few leashes, but if you're setting up as a dog-coat maker then you'll need somewhere to store all the products and packaging. The chances are that this will be your own home so always consider the logistical implications.

Approaching a new business is very much about looking at all the ways it could go wrong – but this doesn't mean approaching it negatively. If you can weigh up the risks and make sure that you can live with them, then you can go about your enterprise with no buried anxieties holding you back.

LIFE IN LIMBO

HOW TO COPE WITH UNCERTAINTY

After a lifetime of work, many of us would like to think we'd earned some certainty in our lives. How do you deal with it when retirement looks even more uncertain than your old life?

You may be able to build up savings and establish a decent pension or some investments, but there's still a wild card: you're budgeting for an unknown period of time. You might have decades of life still ahead of you – which is doubtless the better option, but it's also the option that needs more money. Especially if you live in a country where medical costs aren't covered by the state.

Does money matter?

Exactly how to manage this will depend on where you live: your best bet is to consult a financial adviser (see pp100–01) and discuss what kinds of pension plan and insurance would be least stressful. That said, it may be reassuring to know that according to a study by Nobel laureate Daniel Kahneman, the idea that money equals happiness is "largely illusory" – as long as you're not actually starving, your day-to-day happiness isn't greater for having money. In fact, a review by the Stanford Graduate School of Business found the cycle of buying new material things can cause more stress than it cures. It's relationships that really make us happy.

Happy at home?

If relationships are the key to happiness, do you feel confident or uncertain about yours? If you're married, do you and your partner have similar ideas about how to spend your retired days? In particular, how much time do you want to spend together? As the *Journal of Estate Planning* heard one succinct spouse declare: "Look, I said I'd take you for better or worse, but I didn't say I'd take you for lunch every day." Relationship conversations can be just as high-stakes as money conversations, so try to discuss your expectations.

Those of us without partners or children may need to be more strategic about planning to see friends and relations. Being single can also cause an extra financial strain: retirement coach Jacob Gold recommends joining investment clubs as a "fantastic" way to get practical help and

social contact at the same time. If you're single (or even if you're not), it may be smart to discuss plans for companionship with your platonic friends: that way, drifting apart becomes less likely.

Practice makes perfect
Meanwhile, what are your family's plans? Are your friends going to stay nearby or retire overseas? Have you tried out the activities and schemes you're planning to do yet? These are things you may need to practise to put yourself at ease with them; as Canadian psychologist John Osborne puts it, "Taking several years prior to retirement to build what will become a retirement lifestyle can make the transition less problematic."

READY AND WAITING?
How likely are you to be **financially prepared?** It may depend on your life circumstances. A 2014 study by the RAND Corporation found the number of people who **didn't have enough savings** for retirement was:

20%
OF MARRIED COUPLES

35%
OF SINGLE MEN

49%
OF SINGLE WOMEN

Q BALANCING STRESS

A bit of anxiety when facing a life change is normal, but how much are you likely to worry? Researchers at Duke University in North Carolina argue that four factors are at play:

1 **Flexibility**: are you a go-with-the-flow sort of person, or do changes bother you?

2 **Support**: isolation makes it harder for everyone; more support means more confidence in adapting to new situations.

3 **Confidence**: if you have a general sense of wellbeing and self-esteem, you're likely to feel more able to face the unknown.

4 **Satisfaction**: do you feel your life is meaningful, or are you a bit lost? Getting a sense of purpose can guide us through uncertain times.

If you know that one or more of these isn't your strong suit, you should practise cultivating them ahead of retirement.

PLANNING WHO YOU'LL BE
LEARNING FROM ROLE MODELS

Role models aren't just for children. Retirement involves a change of identity – so when you think about who you want to be, try considering whom you might want to be like.

Many of us find it hard to picture retirement. We've experienced holidays or, perhaps, periods of unemployment, but neither are a good model: one is a temporary break and needs no real structure or planning to be fun, while the other is a period of stress you want to end as soon as possible. Retirement, in contrast, is an open-ended arrangement. As people who've probably spent our lives first in school and then work, how do we approach a long-term identity without definite tasks?

Watch and learn
One thing we can learn from school and work is the importance of mentors and role models. If you think back, you'll probably agree

that watching and learning from older kids at school or from senior colleagues at work gave you a psychological advantage: even if they didn't directly mentor you, just observing them as they went about their business was a useful lesson in how a successful person

> **Role models**, whether they are active in our lives or not, provide a path to living a **positive and meaningful life**.
>
> **Cathy Severson**
> Retirement counsellor

could be. Retirement is a less-structured environment, so you may have to cast around a little more to find similar role models, but it's still a useful trick.

Get listing
Counsellor Cathy Serverson of Retire WOW advises making a list of people, including respected elders from your own life and "public people who have aged admirably". For each individual, write down the qualities that have made them so impressive in their later years, and then consider which of those qualities you share. There may be more than you think.

Applying the theory
As well as identifying real life role models, applying a psychological model to your retirement (see opposite) can give you a sense of satisfaction and legitimacy. Whether you're planning to steam through retirement with

STARS IN THEIR EYES

In 2011, **1,964 US citizens** either just before or just after retirement were asked **which celebrity** they'd most like to model themselves on. The most popular choice was **Betty White** – chosen by 34 per cent of respondents. Why? Because she **"knows how to laugh"**.

all pistons firing or are looking for a quiet life, having a model might help silence any nagging voices in your head (or, indeed, in your family) telling you that you should be doing something more pro-active or restful. It's also another way of identifying individual role models: if you feel, for example, that the "searcher" life – as described in the model (see right) – is for you, you can look around for successful searchers and see what you can learn from them.

Above all, look for happy retirees. Just seeing how much enjoyment people can experience is a model in itself: it lets us know it's possible and gives us psychological permission to do the same.

ARE YOU AN ADVENTURER OR A CONTINUER?

As you plan your retirement, it might be helpful to apply a theory proposed by counselling psychologist Nancy K. Schlossberg, EdD. In her "psychological portfolio", Schlossberg identified six different types of retiree:

Continuers
People who base their activities on skills and interests they've already developed.

Easy gliders
People who just enjoy the freedom that an unscheduled day allows.

Retreaters
People who want a break from it all – they disengage or at least take some time out.

Adventurers
People who launch into entirely new enterprises.

Searchers
People who adopt a trial-and-error approach as they look into new possibilities.

Involved spectators
People who may be less actively engaged than before, but are still emotionally invested in what's happening in the world.

Which of these psychological models sounds like the best approach for you? There's probably no one "best" answer – you can be a happy or unhappy version of each – but it might be helpful to know which one feels most appropriate.

KNOWING WHO YOU ARE

WORK AND IDENTITY

The transition from "person who does job X" to "retired person" is a major one for the self-image to absorb. The best time to start adjusting to the new you is in the lead up to retirement.

Even if you don't always enjoy work, it can provide a sense of purpose and self-esteem. When the time comes to think about stopping, it can be easy to assume that you'll still feel like yourself, just with more free time. In fact, it can be a surprisingly difficult change to handle. In preparation, a year or so before you leave, start identifying exactly how work rewards you psychologically. That way, you can see how to replace those rewards in retirement.

In it for the status?

We live in a world that places a high value on work. Retirement, on the other hand, can make you feel like something of a "has-been".

Why do we want status? In his book *Status Anxiety*, the philosopher Alain de Botton proposes that we're motivated less by the intrinsic appeal of wealth or power than by "the amount of love we stand to receive as a consequence of high status". When you picture yourself as a successful member of the working world, what do you imagine other people are thinking about you that makes you a "success"? Is it, for example, your competence, contribution to society, cleverness, or loyalty? When you know what makes you feel the most loveable – and the most loved – it can be a great guide to what activities you might find rewarding in retirement.

WHAT MAKES YOU TICK?

To find out what gives you the greatest sense of usefulness at work, try keeping a daily diary. List your activities throughout the working day and decide how each activity supports your sense of the skills and aptitudes below. Rate activities on a scale of 1 (no support) to 5 (a lot of support). Think about which skills and aptitudes make you feel best about yourself.

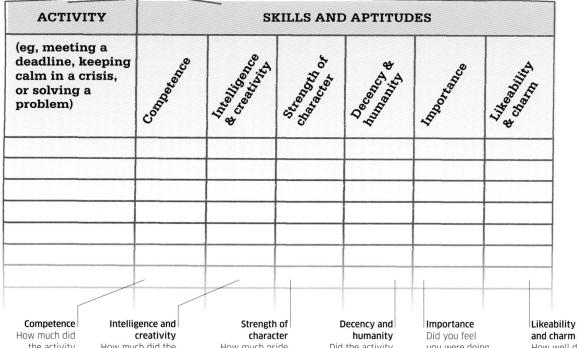

ACTIVITY	SKILLS AND APTITUDES					
(eg, meeting a deadline, keeping calm in a crisis, or solving a problem)	Competence	Intelligence & creativity	Strength of character	Decency & humanity	Importance	Likeability & charm

Competence
How much did the activity make you feel like a skilled, organized, intelligent, accomplished, or sensible person?

Intelligence and creativity
How much did the activity challenge and reward your capacity for higher thought, eg solving a problem?

Strength of character
How much pride did you take in the activity, eg could you stand by your principles or support others?

Decency and humanity
Did the activity make you feel like you were making the world a better place, eg choosing an ethical option?

Importance
Did you feel you were doing something worthwhile, either for yourself or as part of a greater whole?

Likeability and charm
How well did you get along with others during the activity, either casually or in a close friendship?

Feeling useful?

The great thing about retirement is that you can do things that reflect your own values rather than dedicating yourself to a job that might or might not strike you as rich in meaning. As you approach retirement, make a list of which activities give you the greatest sense of usefulness (see above). In retirement, creative or volunteer activities might give you the same feeling, or you may want to look for a new, more manageable kind of job, but either way, you'll be better informed about your own needs.

Ready to try something new?
Rating your aptitudes and skills (see above) might give you some ideas about suitable new avenues to explore in retirement. There are plenty of online tests to take, too – try searching under "career assessment".

CHAPTER 3
WHEELS IN MOTION
INTO A NEW DAWN

GOING IN PREPARED
PSYCHOLOGICAL TRANSITIONS

Is retirement the last stage of life? Probably not, in fact: it's very likely that it will have stages within stages, and you'll have more rites of passage to undergo before you're through.

In the 1970s, the US sociologist Robert Atchley first proposed his theory of retirement, which he continued to refine over the subsequent 30 years. Atchley's idea was simple, and yet counter to how many of us still think about retirement: retirement is a process, not an event.

After you've left your job, you still have a life to live – and you continue to evolve and adapt just as you did before. You'll still be the same person, and how you were before will show "continuity" – that is, it will keep influencing how you think and react. However, there are some common phases that Atchley identified that might be useful to think about before you take the step. He himself acknowledged that everyone is an individual and no one follows the template exactly, but try it on for size and see if it sounds likely for you.

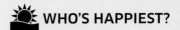 **WHO'S HAPPIEST?**

According to a US study in 2004, the people who felt most comfortable as they moved through Atchley's phases of retirement (see opposite) were those with higher self-esteem, which, perhaps, is hardly surprising. People who thought of themselves as good friends were also likely to be happier: retirement gave them the opportunity to act on that identity more readily.

Q THE SIX PHASES OF RETIREMENT

PHASE 1: PRE-RETIREMENT

You start to disengage from your job and focus more on plans for the future (the stage this chapter covers in more detail).

PHASE 2: RETIREMENT

In the period immediately after retirement, Atchley identified three common types:

- **The "honeymooner"**: you feel like it's a holiday and get active with all the recreation you didn't have time for before.

- **The "immediate routine" retiree**: if you already had a stable schedule outside of your job, you simply expand it until it fills all your time.

- **The "rest and relaxation" retiree**: while a honeymooner is busy, you prefer to do nothing too demanding (often because you're exhausted from a hectic life at work). People who begin by relaxing often get more active over time.

PHASE 3: DISENCHANTMENT

Some people go through a phase of unhappiness or uncertainty. A big life event such as being widowed or regretting a move can trigger this, but it can also happen once you've gone through the honeymoon or rest period and start feeling the desire to do something else. Luckily, this phase can lead on to...

PHASE 4: REORIENTATION

If you've been feeling disenchanted, you start taking stock and making new plans. Some people get more involved in their community; some move to a more affordable or congenial setting; some take up new activities. Whatever you do, you start setting yourself along a new path.

PHASE 5: RETIREMENT ROUTINE

Some people get here right away, while others have to go the long way round, but this is a positive place. You've tried out this and that, you've discovered what's comfortable and fulfilling, and you finally settle into a structure that can work for years or decades. (This doesn't mean you can't adapt it, of course, but it provides a stable base from which to grow.)

PHASE 6: TERMINATION OF RETIREMENT

Your health starts to fail, and your focus shifts to managing it as comfortably as you can.

? WHAT DOES THIS MEAN FOR ME?

The ultimate goal of retirement, according to Atchley, is not to "stop work" but to establish a new structure that's rewarding in the long-term. You may already have one planned, or there may be some experimentation ahead of you, but if you can view retirement as a period of working towards a chosen structure rather than one imposed by work, you're well on your way.

DOWN WITH LABELS
FINDING A NEW IDENTITY

What you do for a living can come to define you, and even if you don't like the definition, losing it can cause complications for your sense of identity. What are the reasons behind this shift in perception?

We may not be entirely happy with the identity that came with our work – some jobs just sound more exciting than others – but even if you're not really sorry to shed the stuffy or unassuming stereotypes that went with your career, being identified as a "retired person" might not feel too thrilling either. Most people ask, "So what do you do?" as a first move when chatting with a stranger, and even if your job title wasn't exactly how you thought of yourself, it was, at least, a way to answer the question. Nobody wants to be asked "What do you do?" and have to say "Nothing": it's hardly good for your confidence to define yourself as a doer-of-nothing. How do you identify yourself once your most obvious label has been discarded?

Defining a new identity
It's useful in this context to consider social identity theory. Pioneered by social psychologist Henri Tajfel in 1979, the theory suggests that we define our identities along two different dimensions: the social and the personal. Our social identity is determined by our membership in particular groups, such as nationalities, religions, sports teams – or, of course, jobs. Personal identity is based on what makes us distinct and different from other people. Psychologists disagree about

? A QUESTION OF IDENTITY

It's important to remember that, while we may be familiar with analysing our psyche and identity as individuals, humans are social creatures, and it's healthy to look to our social groups for at least some sense of who we are. A good approach might be to ask yourself the following two key questions:

Q Do I have enough groups in my life to make up a sense of social identity?

A s you approach retirement, you might start to feel yourself being shunted into an unwanted social identity – "old person" and "person who does nothing" being two common, negative examples. To avoid placing yourself in such categories, or being placed there by others, it's a good idea to find your own, new groups – be it through new work, hobbies, or family time.

Q Who are my main points of comparison when I think of my personal identity?

A If you mostly compare yourself with work colleagues – even colleagues you didn't like might have been a bracing example of who *not* to be – then the next question is: who might stand in for them? Maybe the memory of their character is enough, or perhaps you might want to look around for new people in your post-retirement life.

Retirement, if you approach it cannily, needn't be a loss of identity so much as a chance to reconsider and choose your own definitions this time.

whether social and personal are opposite ends of a spectrum or whether they're interconnected; after all, personal identity means comparing ourselves with others, and the groups we join give us people to compare ourselves with. What's different about us in one group might be a common quality in another one. Regardless, it's helpful to bear these categories in mind when considering the psychological impact of retirement.

Leaving a work-based group can create something of a gap. If you always strongly relied on your membership of non-job-based groups, or your sense of personal identity was defined against a broad range of people, you may have more of a psychological safety net. However, work is where we spend most of our time, so even if you're a robust sort of person, chances are you'll have to do at least a little rethinking.

⏱ THE "ELDERLY" LABEL

Why is 65 supposed to be the age of retirement, despite really not feeling that old these days? You can thank Otto von Bismarck (the first chancellor of a united Germany), who in the 1880s devised Europe's first pension plan. At the time, the life expectancy in Europe and the USA was only 45. Times change, however, and the idea that retirement simply means "old age" is a century and a half out of date.

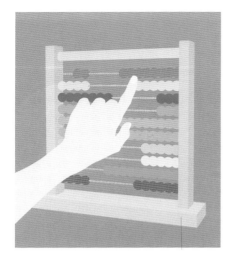

FINALIZING FINANCE
KEEPING ON TOP OF CASHFLOW

Most of us dread the thought of running out of money in retirement. To avoid that fate, what areas do you need to pay close attention to when making your retirement plans?

Retirement requires us to make a long-term financial plan. For some of us this may be straightforward, but for many, it can seem like a lot to take on. How do you manage the complications?

Getting the right advice
A few consultations with an expert might be the smartest investment you can make. The question is, how do you find someone you can trust?

Your bank is not the best place to start: however well-intentioned the staff, it's their job to promote their own services, and they're unlikely to give you a complete picture. What you want is someone independent, whose only professional commitment is to their clients – ie you. A recommendation can be the simplest method: if someone whose judgment you respect has a good financial adviser, you could simply ask for their number. (It's better if they've known that adviser for long enough to be sure that they really are competent, not just plausible.) There's nothing unprofessional about this: most good independent financial advisers get their clients by recommendation.

If you don't have a reliable recommendation to go on, it's time to shop around. Here are the key questions to ask:

■ What are the adviser's hourly rates? They should be clear and fair. (Avoid advisers who work on commission.)

■ What professional qualifications and memberships do they have? In many nations there are professional bodies to which a reputable adviser should belong, so check out their accreditation before you proceed.

■ Do they have ties to any company? If so, this will compromise how many options they can recommend to you.

■ Is their advice clear? An adviser who relies on jargon is no good; you need someone who makes sure you understand – possibly even providing you with a sample plan so you can see what you'd be getting if you signed up with them.

■ Are you comfortable with him or her? Nobody makes their best decisions when they're ill-at-ease: choose someone you like, who will be in contact as much as you need, and who doesn't pressure you.

WARNING FLAGS

What expenses might hit you once you leave work? Retirement adviser Dave Bernard recommends taking five basic areas into account:

1 Healthcare costs
Can you rely on public healthcare, or do you need insurance – and if so, just how much does it cover?

2 Basic living expenses
Food shopping, utility bills, regular travel expenses, and so on: it's useful to have a clear estimate of what these will be.

3 Recreational expenses
Travel, keeping up a club membership, fine dining, hobbies: retirement should be fun, so try to budget for some pleasure spending.

4 Unforeseen expenses
A relation has a crisis, the roof springs a leak, the car breaks down: these are things that mean you'll need a financial cushion.

5 Miscellaneous expenses
Do you have a particular hobby or interest that will need some cash to keep it alive? Budget for it.

TO RENT OR NOT TO RENT?

If you're planning to free up funds by downsizing, does this mean you have to buy somewhere new or could you rent instead? Here are the pros and cons:

Advantages of renting	Advantages of owning
■ Frees up a lump sum.	■ More control and independence.
■ Lets you relocate easily if, say, your children move away.	■ If house prices rise, you won't be shut out of the market (although of course, you may take a hit if prices fall).
■ Saves you tax on buying somewhere new.	■ All money paid on mortgage or maintenance is an investment.
■ Your landlord is responsible for maintenance.	■ If your mortgage is paid off, there's a greater sense of financial security.
■ If you're concerned about declining health, you can choose a home specifically with disability access in mind.	■ It's an asset to leave to your kids.

SAFE AS HOUSES?

The AARP (formerly the American Association of Retired Persons) reported in 2014 that **rates of home ownership** are dropping in **younger retirees**:

80%

...of **over-65s** were home-owners. compared with only....

76%

...of **55–64-year-olds**.

RETIREMENT HAS THE POTENTIAL TO BE LESS OF A 'WITHDRAWAL FROM' THAN A 'RELEASE TO'

JUDITH MALETTE AND LUIS OLIVER
CLINICAL PSYCHOLOGISTS

PLAYING THE ENDGAME
YOUR FINAL CONTRIBUTION

You've made the decision; you know you'll soon be leaving work. Until that final day, however, you still want to contribute meaningfully in your workplace – so how do you stay engaged?

It's one thing to stay committed to a job when it represents your future. As you come up to the day of retirement, however, your workplace is increasingly part of your past. It's a delicate psychological balance to strike: you want to stay motivated enough not to just be spinning your wheels, but not so involved that you can't bear the thought of leaving. What's the best solution?

Announcing your departure
The atmosphere around you can change once people know you'll be leaving soon. Of course, if you're approaching retirement age your co-workers will always know it's a possibility, but there's a difference between "probably leaving in the next few years"

STAYING CREATIVE

Whether or not your job demands much imagination, you'll want to keep your mind fertile – both to stay interested in your last months at work and to take you into retirement. Creativity expert Professor Keith Sawyer suggests the following exercise for over-50s to keep your mind out of a rut: draw objects that are two things at once – a piece of furniture that's also a fruit, a vehicle that's a fish, or a lampshade that's a book. Even if you're no artist, making your brain picture strange combinations keeps it open to possibilities.

and "definitely leaving five weeks from today". If you've long been the sole expert on something, you may find people pumping you for all the information they can get, but it's also possible that your colleagues might start to detach a bit. Hopefully they won't drift away emotionally if they're your friends, but for those people you're less close to, there's a practical consideration: getting too involved in a team they know will break up before the finish line isn't the most attractive idea, and people may prefer to take their new ideas to colleagues they know will be around for the long haul.

Timing it right

When it comes to letting people know you're going, it's important to pick your moment carefully. Assuming your employer can keep a secret, you might choose to wait a while between finishing retirement negotiations with them and telling everybody else. Have a think about how your colleagues are likely to react, and do whatever seems likely to bring about the happiest option.

SEEKING MOTIVATION

How can you stay motivated at work when you're halfway out of the door? Whether or not your colleagues keep you involved is likely to affect your motivation – we're more likely to be motivated to help those who help us – but there's also the question of motivation in general. After all, you might not be around to see the completion of the projects you're currently working on: do you really care that much any more?

It's dull to work without caring, so if you can find reasons to stay interested, it'll probably be better for you. A European study in 2007 noted that, while younger workers are more interested in jobs that offer challenge, variety, and feedback, older workers are more motivated by "intrinsic factors or internal rewards" – that is, whether the work itself feels satisfying to do. We might conclude that younger workers are looking to prove themselves, whereas those of us who've been in the workforce for some time – and who've given plenty of proof of our abilities already – may be more motivated by focusing on what it is about the job that we actually enjoy. If it's within your control, it's a good idea to proactively seek out and volunteer for the tasks you like the best. You may well do this anyway, but your co-workers might be a little more amenable to requests if you're known to be leaving.

It'll be a period of readjustment: we're encouraged to have our "eyes on the prize", and now it's time for you to shift focus. The best thing, in the end, might be to think of the prize as the enjoyment of the work, rather than a long-term goal.

DON'T FORGET VACATION DAYS

Holiday allowance is part of your contract, so either take a pre-retirement holiday or negotiate compensation for it before you fix on a leaving date – otherwise the days might get lost, leaving you short-changed. One good use of the time might be to treat them as an experiment period: take a break shortly before you leave for good to try out some of your planned retirement activities.

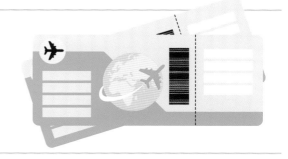

BRING IT ON

CHANGE AND PERSONALITY

Are you ready for change? The answer may lie not just in your attitude to work and how you'll feel when you leave, but also in your personality. Who among us is most comfortable with new circumstances?

C an a person know how they'll feel about a big change in their life beforehand? If you think that the only answer is to wait and see, you could be underestimating psychology a little. Instead, ask yourself this: what sort of personality do I have?

The right character?

One of the most popular theories in the psychology of personality is the "five factor model", which measures people on five different personality traits (see opposite). The main point is this: we all have these qualities in greater or lesser degrees, and how much we have of each trait – and how they interact with each other – can tell you a lot about a person.

A study conducted in the UK in 2010 measured how these factors related to life satisfaction before and after retirement. Personality is, of course, a complicated thing, but there were some notable findings.

Firstly, it found that extroverted people were likely to be happier while in work – a time when networking is a useful skill – but after retirement introverts and extroverts were about equally contented. The researchers speculated that extroversion might mean a bigger social circle, making for good support that protects extroverts from a drop-off in retirement. On the other hand, introverted people tend to be quite happy with a few intimate friends and don't feel the need for a large group of acquaintances,

and that can be established before retirement too. The good news is that once you've retired, it doesn't really matter whether you're outgoing or private: your chances of happiness are equally good.

The same is true of how open to new experiences people are – good news for those who fear that retirement equals stagnation, as it suggests the more adventurous retirees won't feel bored.

Worried or satisfied?

Unsurprisingly, people who scored highly for neuroticism in the study reported being less happy about retirement and were more prone to struggling with the transition. Since neuroticism is essentially a measure of how vulnerable you are to negative feelings, it's not unexpected that people with a high degree of the quality would feel apprehensive about it. There's nothing wrong with being a bit neurotic, but if that sounds like you, the study

? WHAT ARE THE FIVE FACTORS OF PERSONALITY?

The following headings describe the key personality traits that people have, to greater or lesser degrees. Each factor is viewed not as an either/or, but as a scale; our personality depends on which end of the spectrum we gravitate towards. While some of the terms may sound value-heavy - for example, a person with low agreeableness might have good leadership qualities - your level on each of the factors can make it easier or harder for you to feel comfortable in certain situations.

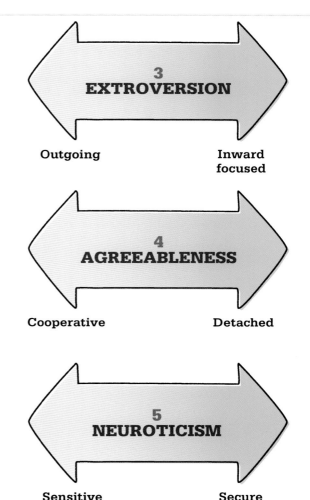

3 EXTROVERSION

Outgoing   Inward focused

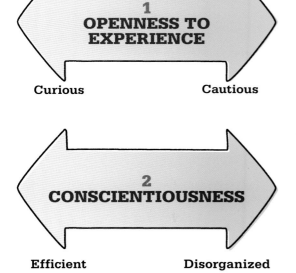

1 OPENNESS TO EXPERIENCE

Curious   Cautious

4 AGREEABLENESS

Cooperative   Detached

2 CONSCIENTIOUSNESS

Efficient   Disorganized

5 NEUROTICISM

Sensitive   Secure

suggests it's important to make sure you have good support: change can be stressful and neurotic people are easily stressed.

The strongest indicators of satisfaction in retirement, however, were conscientiousness and agreeableness. The latter quality seems logical enough – agreeable people tend to have more friends, and social support makes retirement a nicer place – but what about conscientiousness? The researchers speculated that people who planned and organized were actually better able to do so post-retirement: in a job, you don't usually control your own schedule, but once you're in a more "self-determined" position, as the researchers put it, those skills come into their own, and you can use them to arrange things to please yourself. It turns out that for someone of an organized and dutiful disposition, retirement is often a change for the better.

TOWARDS THE HORIZON
MANAGING YOUR EXPECTATIONS

As you approach the big day, you'll benefit from cultivating a balance of optimism, wariness, and realism: that way, you can start your new life in a more robust state of mind.

Our sense of ourselves isn't built just on who we are right now but also on our expectations for the future: what is confidence, after all, if not a tendency to predict that things will work out OK? When it comes to retirement, we're likely to feel better if we have at least some confidence – but on the other hand, there are few things worse for your self-esteem than building up expectations only to have them dashed. As you move into the transition to retirement, how do you keep positive but realistic?

Practical perspectives

Life can hit us with unexpected issues: sudden expenses, health crises, things we can't anticipate. Visiting a doctor and a financial adviser are the best way to make sure that your expectations are at least well-informed.

If you're inclined to procrastinate, make your bookings in stages. Put a note in your diary for the first step: next Monday you'll spend an hour researching advisors; next Wednesday you'll call the doctor. That gives you time to work up to it – or, indeed, to create enough anticipation that you start to look forward to having it over with.

People in mind

At weekends or on holidays we get to see our family and friends, so it's natural to think of retirement as the period of life in which we do that a lot. However, it's very possible that they won't be around as much as you'd like, which can be disappointing – especially as you're dealing with the first few weeks at home, when your new routines aren't set up and you're at risk of feeling lonely.

You may also miss your work colleagues; some friendships do outlast the working environment, but realistically the thing you and your co-workers most had in common – your workplace – has now changed. There's no reason to despair of those friendships, but it is a good idea to remember that they may need a new centrepoint, such as a shared activity.

Time on your hands
You may find yourself with more time on your hands than you expected. When we're working, it can feel like we seldom have time for all the fun we'd like. However, we build our recreation around the time available to us. Just because a weekend wasn't enough to fit in all the fun we wanted, that fun won't necessarily fill a whole week.

The best advice is to expect a teething period. Some things – be they finances or friendships – are best preserved if you anticipate a few strains and do as much as you can in advance to ease them along.

IS IT DIFFERENT ON THE OTHER SIDE?
A 2012 poll by BlackRock and Boston Research Group of both **pre- and post-retirees** found the following divergences between **expectation and reality**:

Retirement age

48% ...of workers expected to keep working **past 64**.

17% ...of workers expected **never to retire** at all.

81% ...of retirees had in fact stopped working **before reaching 64**.

Retirement finances

34% ...of workers anticipated doing some **paid work in retirement**.

15% ...of workers anticipated needing to **work out of necessity** in retirement.

86% ...of retirees didn't in fact receive **any income from work**.

This isn't necessarily bad news – those not earning in retirement weren't all impoverished, for example – but it does suggest that it pays to make a conservative estimate of things.

TRICKY TIMES
Financially speaking, recent years haven't been kind to most of us, with the majority of the "baby boomer" generation (born between 1946 and 1964) feeling insecure about their future. Help may lie in finding a financial adviser (see p100). A 2014 study by the Insured Retirement Institute found that people's confidence about retirement more than doubled if they'd spoken to a professional:

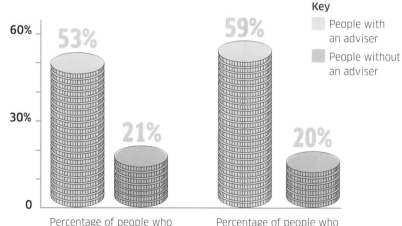

Key
People with an adviser
People without an adviser

53% — Percentage of people who were "extremely" or "very" confident they were doing a good job preparing financially for retirement.

21%

59% — Percentage of people who were "extremely" or "very" confident they would be able to afford a comfortable life in retirement.

20%

ANTICIPATING THE LOSS
THE FEAR OF MISSING YOUR JOB

As a species, human beings aren't keen on giving things up. Retiring from your job, even if it's the right move for you, can feel like a worrying idea. So are you feeling optimistic, or will you feel bereft?

While not all of us are lucky enough to have a dream career, there's a good chance you'll be feeling some last-minute hesitation at the thought of giving up your job – even if it wasn't quite what you would have chosen. What's going on here?

The endowment effect
In a study conducted in the USA in 1990, three psychologists gave a group of volunteers coffee mugs and asked them to negotiate prices with a second group of volunteers. Subjects with mugs to sell were unwilling to part with them for less than $5.25, while subjects considering buying tended to value the mugs at no more than $2.75. Were they just haggling? Perhaps – but we're equally inconsistent when it comes to more emotional issues. In his book *Predictably Irrational*, psychologist Dan Ariely describes how 13 couples travelled to China to adopt new daughters from an orphanage. They all marvelled at the wisdom of the orphanage director who "matched" the perfect child to each couple. In fact, the matches were made at random, and the couples had simply fallen in love with whichever daughter chance had given them.

These episodes are examples of the "endowment effect": a tendency to value something more highly purely because it's ours. It can work for coffee mugs, it can work for family members – and it can work for jobs. The chances are that the very fact your job is yours has endowed it, in your private psychology, with greater value.

How do we detach?
Can we reduce the pull of the familiar? Recent experiments suggest that maybe we can. In 2007, US researchers Owen Jones and Sarah Brosnan decided to test the endowment effect with chimpanzees and found that the apes were just as conservative as people: they wouldn't swap an "endowed" snack for one they would actually have preferred (see opposite). However, the same chimps were more willing to swap when it came to toys. The difference? Food has more "evolutionary salience" – that is, you can survive without a toy much better than without food.

If that's true, the question then becomes: how do you value your job? If you view it as a source of

WHO'S MOST INVESTED?

A US experiment conducted in 2002 asked an interesting question:
what kinds of attachment to our jobs make us most reluctant to leave?
The findings, detailed below, were intriguing:

Type of attachment	Definition	You might say...	Willingness to retire
Job involvement	You value your role as "a lawyer" or "a chef", for example: the identity it gives you feels important.	"I'm an accountant; I'm smart and professional." "I'm a police officer; I keep people safe."	Surprisingly, **more willing**. The researchers speculated that these people were either burning out at work or were equally "involved" in their retirement plans.
Company identification	You value feeling involved in your particular organization.	"I love working for the local council; we're central to the community." "This firm is high-flying – it's great to be part of that."	**Less willing**. These people were slightly more eager to stay on at work.
Professional attachment	You value being part of a particular profession.	"Scientists make the world go round." "Teachers are the backbone of the country."	**Ambivalent**. The researchers noted, however, that some of these people may have had plans to do more work after retirement.

money and community, things you can't do without, it will be harder to let go of than if you've managed to identify other sources of these essential elements. Consider what your job represents to you and take stock of your retirement plans: the more you can view other aspects of life as truly "salient", the easier it will be to feel that your job is something you can move beyond.

IRRATIONAL SNACKS?

When researchers gave chimpanzees a free choice between peanut butter and fruit juice, **60 per cent** of them preferred juice. However, when they were "endowed" (see opposite) with peanut butter, **80 per cent** of the apes refused to trade it – even though some of them probably preferred the juice.

BETTER TOGETHER

REINFORCING THE NETWORK

Few things are more depressing than loneliness. Now you're coming up to a time in which you won't see the regular round of faces, how do you keep your social circle active?

One of the best things about retirement is that you can choose your own companions. One of the drawbacks, however, is that you have to *find* your own companions – and that can take a bit of work.

Making time for friends

Some people have been in our lives for decades; even if we don't see them often, we know they're part of us. Well, now is the time to see them more. If they're still working they may have less time to socialize, and if they're already retired they may need reminding that you're free now, but either way, you stand only to gain by taking the initiative. Retirement frees us up to be hosts, so why not issue some invitations?

LITTLE CIRCLES

How many friends do you actually need? According to a commonly quoted statistic, **in retirement our social network shrinks to just 9.5 people** on average – but if they're the right nine-and-a-half friends, that might be just fine for you.

Rediscovering old friends

As we get older, people who share early memories become more important to us. If you've drifted apart from someone, getting back in touch can feel embarrassing, but the point where you retire is actually a very good opportunity to overcome any shyness. Social networking sites are big business and people of all ages are using them, so old friends are easier to track down than they've ever been: a message saying "Hey, I've just retired and was hoping to catch up with old friends" might be just what they'd love to hear.

A question of gender?

Men are often expected to be "strong and silent", which doesn't always make it easy to sustain relationships in retirement. This isn't to say that they are emotional illiterates, but heterosexual married men, ask yourselves this: if your wife stopped networking, do you feel confident about your ability to stay in touch with people?

In the end, men and women can learn from each other. Women get a lifetime of practising bonding over mutual affirmation (watch two female retirees admiring photos of each others' grandchildren), and it can be helpful for men to enjoy some open affirmation, too. Meanwhile, shared activities are a traditionally "male" way to be friends, but there's no reason why women shouldn't find activities to share with people they like.

(?) ANYONE FOR DINNER?

Want to entertain but not feeling up to it? Take a tip from that other exhausted demographic: mothers of young children. Canadian writer Kelley Powell started a trend with her tips for hosting what she called the "crappy dinner". The idea is to save your energy for the thing you actually care about: seeing your friends. Here are the rules:

1
No housework before the guests arrive.

2
The menu must be simple – so no special shopping.

3
Wear whatever you'd normally wear.

4
No gifts.

You might prefer a more cultivated name for it depending on personal preference, but if you start the ball rolling, these events can catch on.

Making new friends

Retirees are often advised to take up new hobbies. One reason for this is because a lot of friendships are "situational": the simple fact of being in the same place doing the same thing is the bonding agent – or at least, what gets the friendship started. When considering new hobbies and clubs, ask yourself if they attract the kind of person you'd like to know. Go to one or two events before you leap to a conclusion, however. The senior bungie-jumping club might turn out to be a load of old fogies while the fun people are unexpectedly hanging out at the bonsai appreciation society; you never know till you try.

CASTING OFF
THE ART OF LETTING GO

Few jobs are ever likely to feel completely "finished": our involvement in them goes deep into our identity, and closing the chapter can be difficult. Why is it hard to let go, and what can we do about it?

While it would be nice if every retirement began with a neat handover – tasks wrapped up, farewells cordial, nothing left to worry about – realistically at least some people will retire with a sense of dissatisfaction at not being able to leave everything settled. Why does this nag at us so much?

The Zeigarnik effect

We don't like leaving tasks unfinished – even when we're technically "done". In 1927, Russian psychologist Bluma Zeigarnik noticed that restaurant waiters had a tendency to remember only the orders they hadn't served yet. Testing her theory in a formal experiment, she found that her volunteers had the same experience: interrupt someone halfway through otherwise forgettable tasks (solving simple puzzles in her test), and they'll find it hard to forget about them.

> **Letting go** means [realizing] some people are a **part of your history** but not a part of your destiny.
>
> **Steve Maraboli**
> Motivational speaker

In 1982, US psychologist Kenneth McGraw tested Zeigarnik's findings with an added wrinkle: the subjects had only one puzzle to solve – but it was a hard one. Interrupted before completion with the news that the study was finished, nearly 90 per cent of the subjects kept on trying to solve the puzzle. They were free to go home – but because they weren't finished in their own minds, they didn't want to stop.

When it comes to work, leaving something undone, even when you're free to go, is frustrating. Pay complicates the effect a little (see right), but even so, an unfinished job will probably bother you.

Puzzling people

If you have to leave a project halfway through then you'll almost certainly be feeling troubled by the Zeigarnik effect – but what about unresolved personal issues, such as a dispute you're involved in or trying to mediate? We're social creatures, and if you've dedicated effort and ingenuity to a tricky social dynamic or conflict, leaving that "unfinished" can be even more frustrating than abandoning an intellectual puzzle.

What can you do about this? It might help to think of it like chess: your opponent will be around to make another move after you've gone, so try to make your final move as hard to challenge

Q THINK ABOUT THE MONEY

Does money make a difference when it comes to leaving work undone? In 2006, psychologist Kenneth McGraw followed up his earlier experiment (see left) to see if people would be more willing to leave a task unfinished if they were being paid. Given the opportunity to leave work undone, more of the paid than unpaid subjects walked away – although the majority still tried to finish off. If you're struggling to let go, perhaps you should remind yourself that you've done what you were paid to do: that helped at least some of McGraw's volunteers.

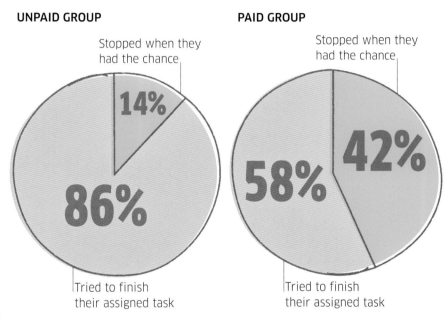

UNPAID GROUP

Stopped when they had the chance
14%

86%

Tried to finish their assigned task

PAID GROUP

Stopped when they had the chance
42%

58%

Tried to finish their assigned task

as possible. With conflict, this means being unimpeachable: you're done, so try to be gracious. As career expert Nicole Williams puts it, "If your level of frustration is high, vent it to your friends and family rather than your co-workers." This won't give you the satisfaction of telling frustrating people what's what, but it will give you the satisfaction of leaving them nothing they can use against you.

Whether it's an ongoing project or conflict, very few of us feel content when we have to leave things undone. If that's happening to you, it might be comforting to reflect that the sheer fact that something is unfinished may be leading you to over-value it. Allow yourself some time and put some completed projects between you and the loose ends – you should find that your natural frustration starts to ease.

SUCCESSFUL DEBRIEFINGS
TOWARDS A SMOOTH HANDOVER

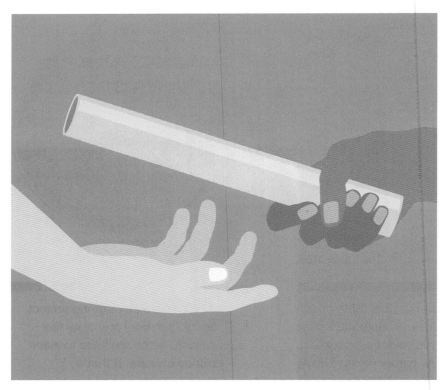

You're about to retire, but others will have to carry on when you leave. What's the most productive way of passing along your knowledge so you can put your mind at ease before you go?

Nobody likes to leave a mess behind them, so how do you make sure your final achievement at work is a satisfactory transition for your successors? Every workplace has its own ideas, but some good ways of smoothing the transition include:

- **Overlapping**: if you're planning a phased retirement (see pp82–83), or if your successor is starting before you leave, that's a good opportunity to work directly with the person or people who'll be taking over your job. You'll be right there for them in case they need any guidance, and you can reassure yourself that they're getting on OK.
- **Fully briefing a junior**: if your successor won't arrive until after you're gone, the "continuity" person in the

Q THE REWARDS OF GENEROSITY

If you're feeling cooperative, the chances are it will be good for your health. A Canadian study in 2014 found that generosity actually kept people healthier. Subjects were given $10 and told they could keep or give away as much as they chose. The more they gave, the lower their levels of cortisol, the stress hormone, became - and lower cortisol levels give us protection against all sorts of afflictions, from cardiovascular disease to cancer. Psychologically speaking, being generous really does seem to bring us major gains.

chain of command is most likely to be the person who assisted you. They may not be able to do your job, but the more you can teach them about how to support the next person, the more confident you (and they) are likely to feel. This is also an opportunity to keep the door open for a while if you feel more comfortable easing out slowly: let the junior know they can call you if they have questions for, say, the first month, and that way you'll either be able to help – or relax in the knowledge that no news is good news.

■ **A written brief**: there are probably things you know that other people won't think to ask until you've gone. If you gather together all the information and pointers you can think of, and leave it as a reference, it will give your successors some guidance and you a sense of closure.

Becoming a mentor

While you yourself may be looking for role models for a happy retirement (see pp90–91), you might also find a lot of satisfaction in acting as a role model for someone else. Some businesses have official mentoring programmes that will allow you to train up your replacement – having the role formally recognized will give you more opportunities to advocate

THE THREE ELEMENTS OF MENTORING

Psychologist Michael Zey describes the following core aspects of mentoring. How these fit into your own workplace will vary from job to job and person to person, but they should help you establish ways of making yourself useful.

1
Teaching: a mentor shows the ropes and gives career guidance.

3
Organizational intervention: a mentor protects his or her protégé when they need it, helps them access resources, and "markets" them – that is, recommends, praises, or otherwise boosts them – to people whose attention might help them along.

2
Personal support: a mentor helps build the protégé's confidence. This doesn't have to be limited to the workplace; a protégé who's having problems with their own life can often benefit a lot from the wisdom and sympathy of a more experienced friend.

for your protégé. However, if your company has no official scheme, it doesn't necessarily rule out becoming a mentor. Essentially, mentoring is a personal relationship, and if you have the right dynamic with any younger co-workers, why not give them some informal support? There are few things more psychologically rewarding than feeling yourself to be a supportive elder to a new generation.

20%

MAKE ME A MENTOR

According to a 2014 survey conducted by the business periodical *HR Magazine*, 20 per cent of all employees polled **wanted to be in a mentoring scheme**.

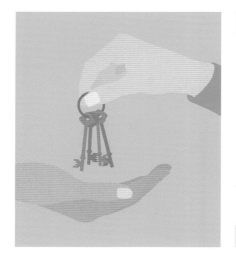

IS MY LEGACY SECURE?
THE SUCCESSION QUESTION

What do you want to leave behind you? Will you simply leave a job well done, or are you in a position to choose your successor? If that is the case, how do you make the right choice?

How much power do you have to choose the new "you" and how do you go about it? Assuming you're in a position to choose and are recruiting from within your own company, the candidates may or may not be obvious: entrepreneur Patrick Ibarra recommends a step-by-step selection process (see opposite).

Either way, ask yourself this: what's non-negotiable and what can change? For example, if your company has an ethical policy you're proud of, then an unscrupulous successor probably isn't acceptable no matter how much acumen he or she has. On the other hand, if you created an aesthetic that made your products successful, is that sacrosanct, or could you accept a talented successor making his or her own changes? It's not always easy to let go, but you're likely to be happier if you focus on preserving the spirit of what you've created rather than the fine details.

Making it personal
Nobody is as good at being you as you – but that doesn't mean they can't be successful in their own way. Psychologically speaking, giving up a position of power is difficult, but mentoring (see p117) is one way to ease the strain: it's nice for your successor to get a supportive handover, of course, but it's also good for you. A protégé's achievements are our own achievements by proxy, while a replacement's successes tend to feel less personal – but whether someone is your protégé or your replacement may partly depend on how you treat them.

Eyes on the prize
Of course, your successor may not always be tactful. US psychologists Harry Levinson and Jerry Wolford talk of the

BRAIN DRAIN
A 2015 survey by the Society for Human Resource Management found that one third of companies were **anticipating staffing problems** as older workers retired and took their expertise with them.

THE PATH TO A SMOOTH HANDOVER

As you identify and prepare to handover to one or more successors, entrepreneur Patrick Ibarra suggests working through the following steps:

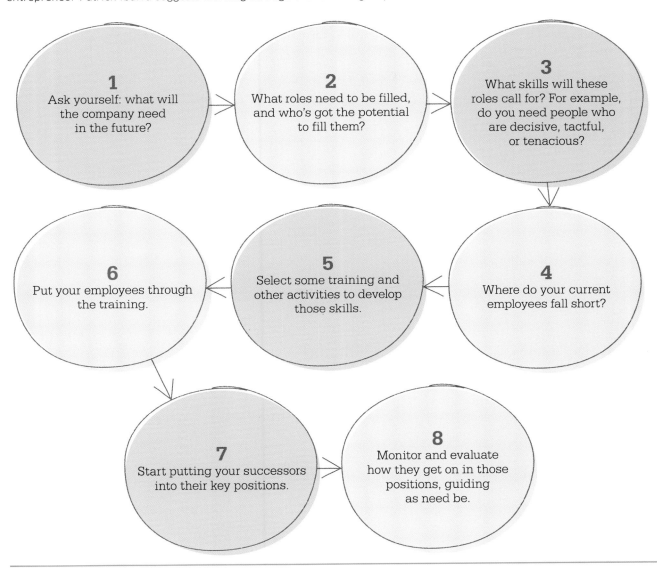

1 Ask yourself: what will the company need in the future?

2 What roles need to be filled, and who's got the potential to fill them?

3 What skills will these roles call for? For example, do you need people who are decisive, tactful, or tenacious?

6 Put your employees through the training.

5 Select some training and other activities to develop those skills.

4 Where do your current employees fall short?

7 Start putting your successors into their key positions.

8 Monitor and evaluate how they get on in those positions, guiding as need be.

"goal gradient hypothesis": the closer people get to a goal, the more tense they feel about not being there yet, and the harder they find it not to jump the gun. If they can resist this urge it will be easier on everyone, but it's best to recognize that there are some situations in which your interests and theirs may be in conflict: you want to set your own pace, while they may be tapping their feet. Concede where you can to minimize their frustration, and remind yourself that they're not really being disloyal: the goal gradient affects us all.

Finding people to replace us isn't easy, but with care and patience you should be able to find individuals you can be proud of.

THOUGHTFUL GOODBYES
THE ART OF FAREWELL

You've decided to leave and your departure is imminent, but how do you deal with all the farewells? No matter how you feel about your colleagues, there are strategies you can use to help you leave in style.

Saying goodbye isn't just a word: when it comes to our psychological wellbeing, it's something closer to a ritual. As anthropologist Krystal D'Costa points out, the word was originally "almost a plea": it's a contraction of "God be with ye", a prayer for someone's safety. In this way, "goodbye" or "farewell" aren't just words we say to other people, they're a way in which we express our own hopes, invoking good wishes by speaking them aloud. "Goodbye" is a word that affects the speaker as much as the hearer. When you're leaving your workplace, you're going to hear yourself saying that word a lot. What will it mean to you?

Friends and workmates

If you are fond of your co-workers and the community you created together, there's no doubt that saying goodbye will be painful, even though you might be moving on to something good. Even if you've built lasting friendships, you won't be sharing the bonding experience of working side by side every day. The social importance of a mutual task is no small thing; in psychology, this is known as a "superordinate goal" – which is to say, something that can't be achieved alone and that requires you to set aside personal differences to achieve it. A superordinate goal can unite very different people; when your fellow-striver is also your friend,

LOST FOR WORDS?

Some of us find words come easily, but others can get a little stuck. What do you say to different people? Make a lasting positive impression with the help of these tips:

Who are they?	What should you say?
Someone you want to stay friends with	■ Talk about how much you've enjoyed their company and support. ■ Make some specific plans. A vague "Let's keep in touch" can be heard as a mere pleasantry; "How about lunch next month?" makes it clear you mean it.
Someone you liked but are happy to let go	■ Talk about what a pleasure it's been working with them, focusing on how you enjoyed the past. This inoffensively conveys the message that you're happy to leave those times behind. ■ Wish them well for the future. That "God be with ye" makes it politely plain that you're trusting them to the Fates rather than involving yourself.
Someone you didn't like	■ Trust to conventional courtesies. Nobody can blame you for using them, and they save you the trouble of worrying what to say. ■ Talk more about their future than your feelings: "Lots of luck" and "Hope it all goes well for you" are less likely to feel like lies. This is probably as true as you'll get: you can hope things go well for them with the silent addendum that "well" should be as far away from you as possible!
Someone you admired	■ Be specific. Tell them they were inspiring or educational, and leave them with the warm feeling that they meant something to you.

it is a real loss when you have to go. You can still be close, of course, but you will be saying goodbye to an era of your friendship, even if you're not saying goodbye to the friend him- or herself. It's worth taking some time to appreciate that.

Letting go of hostility

If you've had conflict with certain workmates, you might feel the temptation to leave with some parting shots. If you can resist that temptation, however, you might be better off aiming to part from them civilly if not warmly.

This isn't just you being the bigger person (although that can be a very satisfying role to assume): it's in your own interests. Studies have found that it's not only stress that increases our chances of heart disease, but hostility as well. Now that you no longer have to work alongside a disliked colleague, their ability to cause you difficulties is about to go away: if you can shake hands and say "Best of luck in the future", it might be literally as well as figuratively good for your heart.

Dealing with departure

Here's a question: how comfortable are you with uncomfortable emotions? Can you ride them out, or do you tend to shut them down? When we want to shield ourselves from the pain of losing something we're attached to, we sometimes do what's called "deactivating": trying to tone down our feelings of fondness by devaluing or finding fault. If you don't really value it, you won't miss it – right?

A little deactivation *can* be helpful if you keep it directed towards things and people you won't be seeing any more, thus easing your psychological transition to retirement. If you're a big deactivator, however, be wary of the temptation to create friction with people you like just to shut down the fear of missing them; it'll only harm your long-term relationships with them.

? TO PARTY OR NOT TO PARTY?

Is yours the kind of workplace that would have a big celebration or a quiet round of drinks after hours on your last day? Is it entirely up to you to organize something? If you have any say in things, what would you prefer?

To begin with, it might be worth considering spacing out some of your farewells. You may or may not have a big celebration coming up, but for closer colleagues it might give you more of a sense of closure if you have several lunches with each of them over the last few weeks. This may appeal to you if you have a number of work friends across different teams, or if you're more of an introvert than an extrovert – you might find it easier to say what you want to say without lots of people around A one-on-one or one-on-two

farewell lunch or drinks is also a good way to convey to fellow workers that they meant something particular to you.

What do we get out of bigger parties? Well, apart from the sense of occasion – and, for retirement parties, the sense of ritual and closure – there's also the psychological effect of being around other people. This effect mostly takes place in the mirror neurons of our brain, which instinctively reflect the feelings of those around us: if you've ever found yourself tearing up when someone was sad, or catching the giggles from someone else, that's your mirror neurons at work. Add some music to give everyone the same emotional soundtrack, so to speak, and a party is at least in part about creating a celebration where people get together to synchronize their emotions.

TIPS FOR CONFIDENCE

Have to make a goodbye speech but dread public speaking? These tips from communication studies professor Paul Witt will help you deal with the symptoms:

Symptom: dry mouth

Solution: keep a cup or bottle of water to hand

Symptom: shaky knees

Solution: flex them and shift your weight around a bit

Q FAREWELL PHOTOS

What does this mean for a retirement party? The main point to remember is that how much you'll enjoy it is likely to depend on how easily the emotions of your fellow workers cohere. If it's a strait-laced workplace where no one really relaxes and you aren't particularly fond of each other, the synchronized emotion is more likely to be awkwardness; a friendly place where no one judges each other is far more likely to create a positive glow.

The chances are that the feeling you'll bring away from the party will be similar to the feeling everyone else was having. Only you can judge whether that will be a dreary let-down or a wonderful gift – but do at least factor it into your thinking and, if a dull party is unavoidable, try to organize some other events that will warm your mirror neurons to counter-balance the dullness. You want to leave in a good mood, so surround yourself with people who'll make that possible.

Want to snap some souvenir shots? Go to it, and have a think about what they'll mean to you later, too. Pictures can often evoke some of the feeling we had when we first took them – or what psychoanalyst Nuar Alsadir calls our "emotional perspective". They don't just record what was in front of us, but by their inclusions and ommissions show something of what we were thinking: where we chose to point the camera, what we "focused" on, what was "central" to us. Keep an eye out for moments that strike you as particularly representative.

Symptom: trembling hands	**Solution:** clasp them together
Symptom: quavering voice	**Solution:** take a deep breath and smile; smiling warms your tone
Symptom: sweating	**Solution:** try to ignore it; you're likely to be much more aware of it than anyone else

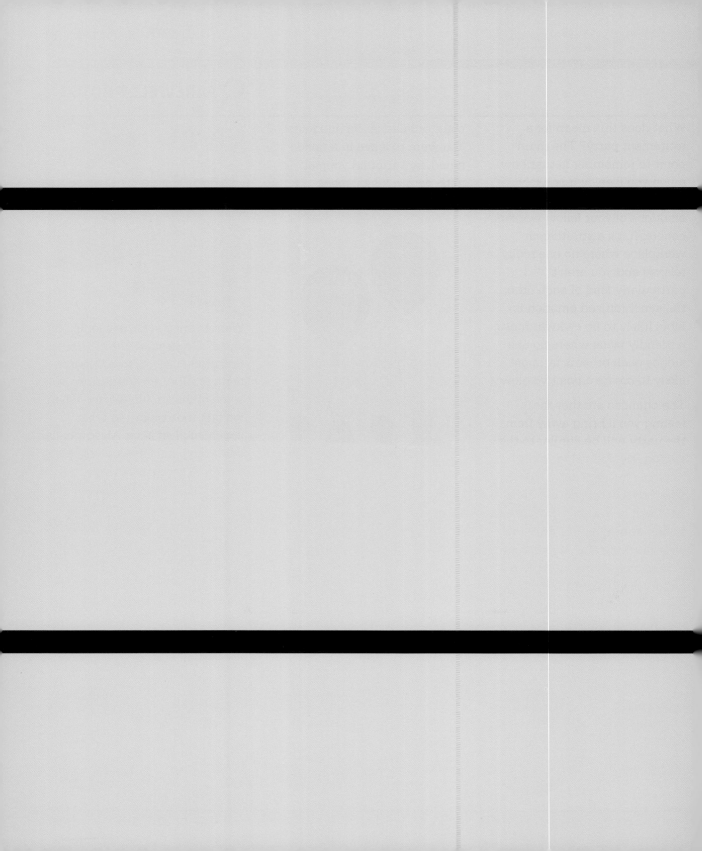

CHAPTER 4

A TIME OF ADJUSTMENT

THE FIRST YEARS OF RETIREMENT

HOME ON A WORK DAY

ADJUSTING TO THE NEW

Even for the most unconventional among us, a routine can be a comforting thing. The early days of retirement, when we either have to create a new routine or do without one, can be a challenge.

It's easy to underestimate the psychological power of the working week and the shape and structure work gives to our days – so much so, in fact, that safety expert Gavin de Becker advises that firing potentially dangerous employees on a Friday afternoon, thus giving them a couple of days to adjust before they find themselves home on a working day, actually reduces the likelihood they'll come back and attack someone. Doubtless you aren't planning a violent rampage, but the new Monday to Friday may still feel a little odd at first. How do you manage that?

A new social life?

Your workmates may not have been your nearest and dearest, but you probably saw them more than those you considered yourself "close" to. Author and

37%

TIME TO COME

If you **retire at the age of 65**, on average you have 37 per cent of your **life still ahead of you**.

> If a **cluttered desk** is a sign of a **cluttered mind**, of what, then, is an **empty desk** a sign?
>
> **Albert Einstein**

psychologist Robert Bornstein comments that it's "not uncommon for people to discover that they have few or no friends" once they hit retirement. This doesn't mean you're unlikeable: in today's global economy, "real friends" often move to other cities or other countries for their jobs, and once you retire, the occasional visit you were able to manage with them starts to seem a bit limited.

How do you deal with this? Getting back in touch with old friends is a great idea (see pp112–13), but it's also wise to start investigating groups that meet in your neighbourhood, such as community projects and local campaigns. Not everyone present may be exactly your type, but probably not all your workmates were your type either – they just happened to be there. While finding close friends, old and new, takes time, finding a regular group that's not ideal but that fills a gap in your life can be a lot quicker.

 THE PSYCHOLOGY OF DECLUTTERING

Many people plan at least some retirement projects, and those projects can call for an office or workroom. We don't all have 20-bedroom mansions, of course, so how do you make space?

You may have a room to spare, you may only be able to set up a desk, but the chances are that you'll need to clear some space. The trouble is that we get sentimentally attached to things that "remind" us of the past, and when you've just retired, that pull may be particularly strong. Do you have to throw everything away? Decluttering is fashionable, but the psychology is actually quite complicated. A 2013 study at the University of Minnesota found that a somewhat messy environment can actually stimulate creative thinking – but another study found that people coming out of a clean environment were more likely to act responsibly: they were more prone to donate to charity, and offered a choice between an apple and a piece of chocolate, were more likely to choose the apple.

What's the solution? Probably it depends on what kind of projects you want to prioritize. A bit of tidying-up is sensible – if it feels overwhelming, commiting to, for example, 15 minutes a day can be a good way to get started – but as Einstein might agree (see left), manageable work or project space is more important than an absolutely pristine one.

The daily grind

According to a 2005 study by the Netherlands Interdisciplinary Demographic Insitute, women tend to report having a harder time adjusting to retirement than men. Why should that be? The researchers posited two explanations: first, that women may find it easier to admit they're struggling; but second, that it's more likely that "the majority of obligations remain unchanged" for someone who's already been responsible for running the home – which is usually a woman. If a change is as good as a rest, women sometimes get less of a change in retirement, and hence feel less psychologically refreshed. If you're part of a heterosexual couple, then it may be that the kindest thing a husband can do for his wife is take on the housekeeping for a while: it's not macho, but it could be profoundly gallant.

UPS AND DOWNS
CHARTING HAPPY PATHWAYS

Mood swings or anxious moments often accompany big life changes – they're an inevitable part of adjusting to a new way of living – and retirement is no exception. So how can we get through the bad days?

Realistically, there are going to be some days when you feel less than positive about yourself. This is true of life in general, but particularly during periods of transition. If you anticipate a certain proportion of "down" moments, you're less likely to panic when they happen. Mixed feelings are normal, and not a sign that anything's going wrong. Still, they're not much fun, so how do you keep them under control?

Areas of happiness
San Francisco-based psychologist Yvette Guererro defines five areas of happiness: satisfiying relationships, mental and physical health, financial security, staying young at heart, and acts of kindness towards others. The key thing with these is to set yourself up for early success: for example, if you're a bit out of shape, start by planning to walk 10,000 steps

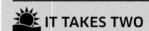 **IT TAKES TWO**

Married, and trying to find a happy balance? Seventy-something psychologist Willard Harley suggests this rule: don't make lifestyle changes, such as starting a new routine or bringing home new friends, without "enthusiastic agreement" between the two of you. It can take negotiation but, as Harley says, "everything you do affects each other". Charting a mutually acceptable course is challenging enough to keep your marriage both fresh and committed.

STIMULATE YOUR SENSES

Having a dark day? Then shine some light on your senses. As clinical psychologist Barbara Serani points out, input from the world around us is just the thing to get our brains going:

Pleasant scents
Pleasant or evocative smells can trigger positive memories and emotions. This is because the olfactory bulb (the scent-processing part of the brain) is part of the brain's limbic system, where emotion and associative learning are processed.

Natural light
The daily cycles of light and dark trigger the release of melatonin – the hormone that controls our "body clock" – from the hypothalamus and pineal gland. Artificial light, especially from phone and computer screens, can disrupt our body's natural rhythms of sleep and wakefulness.

Music and voices
Hearing music and human voices (this can be conversation, but also the radio or an audiobook) encourages the release of dopamine, one of the "feel-good" hormones. Dopamine is produced in several areas of the brain and is released by the hypothalamus.

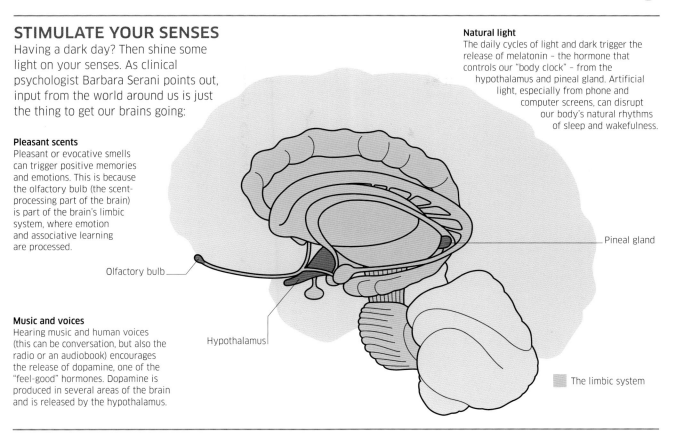

Olfactory bulb

Hypothalamus

Pineal gland

The limbic system

---

a day rather than going straight into a kick-boxing class and giving up when you can't move the next day. Aim for the reachable at first, and then gradually build your ambitions as you build your achievements.

Choosing your goals

Author and inspirational speaker John P. Strelecky suggests creating a "Big Five" list for your retirement: five things that you aim to do, and which will make you feel, as you look back, that you succeeded. These can be finite achievements – visit the Grand Canyon, finally write that paper on your special subject – or they can be ongoing ones, such as "be a loving parent". It's a good idea to have at least one ongoing goal so you don't find yourself stuck after finishing all five. Retirement is a time when you can define success on your own terms, and a list of such goals can be a great way of reminding yourself, during the emotional downswings, that you still have achievements on your horizon.

Dealing with the bad days

Even supposing your plans are perfect and you're doing everything you should, chances are you'll still have some days when all you can think is "What have I got to show for my life?" – how do you cope with those?

Seek out positive sensations to get your brain going (see above). If you have a lot of down days, it may also be a sign that you would do well to create some routines. As author and happiness expert Gretchen Rubin declares, "What you do every day matters more than what you do once in a while." Routines provide predictability and consistency, which lower anxiety, so set up at least some daily activities to keep yourself on track.

FLYING HIGH
MANAGING EUPHORIA

With the daily work routine behind you, you can get a rush of excitement: freedom at last! Of course, we all want to be happy and contented – but can joy be a false friend?

Throughout our lives, we associate freedom from work with pleasure. For most of us, life drops us into a structure of obligations as soon as we enter primary school, and from then on, the only unstructured time we get is limited breaks in which we're free to do whatever we want. You can see this in the words most commonly used to describe these breaks: "vacation", from the Latin "vacationem", meaning "empty" or "free", and "holiday", from "holy day" – we associate freedom from activity with celebration and festivity. When we find ourself looking at the rest of our life after work, it's not surprising that some of us get a little giddy.

Spoilt for choice?

Psychologists have noted that the "honeymoon" phase of retirement tends not to last (see pp96–97): for those of us who really need a break, it's fun to do nothing for a while – but it soon palls. There is an opposite extreme to doing nothing, however: trying to do everything at once. After a lifetime of restraint, it can be tempting to rush ahead without regard for more sober thoughts such as long-term budgeting. Packing each day full of the things you didn't have time for while you were working can be fun for a while, but what was once an exciting novelty, reserved for weekends and holidays may quickly become banal and everyday.

HOW WOULD YOU DESCRIBE YOUR RETIREMENT?

A 2011 study identified four different models – or narratives – of retirement based on the words and phrases used by retirees to describe their new plans and identities. Some models were more consumer-orientated than others, so depending on how much you want – or can afford – to consume, you might like to try on some other "narratives" for size.

My retirement is a time for:	I think of my retirement as:	My retirement "narrative" is:	Likelihood of continuing to work:	Likelihood of spending money:
Exploring new horizons	A transformation, milestone, or renaissance.	Progressive: moving towards a new future.	Low.	High: most likely to spend money on services and activities.
Searching for meaning	A loss or liberation.	Static: focused on the past and present.	Moderate: likely to take on some paid work.	Low.
Contributing on my own terms	A question of staying the course or downshifting.	Focused on the future, but stable.	Moderate: likely to take on paid or unpaid work.	Low.
Putting my feet up	A liberation or downshifting.	Redemptive and in the moment.	Low.	Moderate: retirement is a reward. Most likely to spend on relaxation-based leisure.

Decisions, decisions

Another problem with trying to do too much at once is that we can suffer from what's known as "decision fatigue". US psychologist Jean Twenge, who conducted a study into the phenomenon, concluded that choosing between too many attractive options can leave us less able to resist temptation and more prone to give up. For retirees setting up their future, obviously this has drawbacks: there's every reason to consider a lot of options, but it's prudent to space out the moments of actual payment or signing on the dotted line, just to ensure you don't jump to an unwise choice simply because you've taken on too many decisions at once: empirically, we get worse at choosing the more overloaded with choices we are.

BEYOND THE "HONEYMOON"

A 2013 study in the UK found that retirees become bored, on average, just 10 months after retiring. About one third of respondents felt that "every day ended up being the same", while many said they missed the camaraderie of the workplace. To avoid this feeling, it's vital to plan beyond the "honeymoon" period.

PEACEFUL NIGHTS

SLEEPING WELL OR LYING AWAKE?

Everyone knows we need a good night's sleep to feel all right. But when it comes to retirement and its attendant lifestyle changes, what does a "good night's sleep" actually look like?

When you're working, the regular weeks tend to lay down a clear pattern for "good" sleeping. You get up in the morning when it's time to go to work, you go to bed in the evening early enough to avoid feeling exhausted the next day, and on days off you might catch an extra hour or two's lie-in. After retirement, however, many of us could sleep all day if we chose – and that can be surprisingly disturbing. Between the lack of a formal structure and the natural changes that come with getting older, what sort of sleep schedule should you be aiming for?

Staying healthy

Getting enough rest isn't just a matter of comfort – the right amount can have important health effects. A study presented at the 2012 Alzheimer's Association International Conference found that the ideal amount of sleep for retirees was around seven hours. Those who slept for this long displayed better concentration and memory – meaning they were less vulnerable to cognitive decline – than those who slept less than five or more than nine hours per night.

Of course, some of us tend to be more restless regardless of the circumstances; have a look at the graph (opposite) to see the average pattern for retirees. Most people find their sleep disturbances tend to drop off dramatically just after retirement, usually because the pressures of work have all been concluded – but then, after a few years, their nights start to get more wakeful again.

Disturbed sleep

If you are having restless nights, is it something to worry about? A study published in the *Journal of Behavioural Medicine* suggests that while it may be distressing at times, retirees can often live with restless nights fairly comfortably. The researchers found that they could classify their subjects into three different groups: "good sleepers" (about half the study group); "high distress poor sleepers"; and "low distress poor sleepers". That is, some people slept badly but didn't feel bad about it – and their

10–35%

SLEEPING EASY?

Between 10 and 35 per cent of people over 65 report uncomfortable levels of **sleep disturbance**.

reported levels of wellbeing were quite close to those of the good sleepers. Both the good sleepers and the high distress poor sleepers wanted about seven hours per night: the good sleepers achieved this and the distressed poor sleepers didn't, but their expectations were about the same. The low distress poor sleepers, on the other hand, didn't want that

much; the researchers suggested that they were "naturally short sleepers" who were comfortable with more wakeful nights.

In the early days of your retirement, it's likely that you may want to catch up on some sleep, especially if your departure involved a lot of last-minute organizing that kept you keyed-up and busy. As you start to develop a new routine, however, the evidence suggests that the best plan is to have about seven hours sleep if you can manage it. If you can't, the question becomes, "How much distress is it causing me?" – and if the answer is "a lot", you probably need to check your anxiety levels (see pp134–35) to see if there's a more serious underlying cause.

HOW MUCH SLEEP DISTURBANCE SHOULD YOU EXPECT?

A 2009 international study surveyed nearly 15,000 retirees about their sleep patterns in the years both before and after retirement, and found that disturbances tended to drop off as work worries fell away, but then rose somewhat with age:

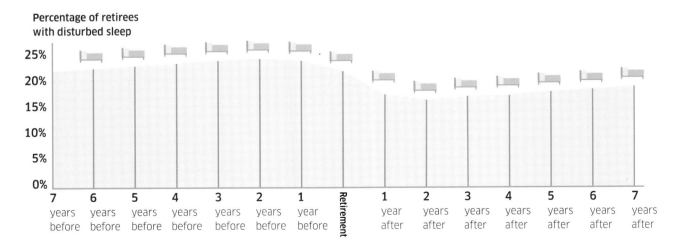

Percentage of retirees with disturbed sleep

STEADY NOW
COPING WITH CHANGE AND ANXIETY

Few of us feel completely calm at the prospect of a major change, with its attendant uncertainties – and retirement is about as major as it gets. How do we keep our anxiety levels in check?

It's likely that you'll be no stranger to retirement nerves even before you leave work. Once you've actually stopped work, however, anxiety levels can shoot up: you no longer have your regular job to distract you from your worries. Dealing with anxiety is extremely important for staying healthy, so what can you do to enhance your sense of calm?

Dealing with change
Anxiety often springs from fear of the unknown. Retirement is a significant life adjustment that involves leaving the supportive social and financial structures you've participated in for most of your life; anxiety is a perfectly natural response to dealing with such unfamiliar circumstances. If you're feeling anxious, take a moment to assess what's worrying you; break your sense of anxiety down into bitesize pieces, rather than letting yourself be overwhelmed by daily nagging feelings.

Taking practical steps
If you're concerned about your finances, what exactly is worrying you? How can you act to mitigate it? Should you hire a professional to help you assess your situation? If you're feeling anxious about family connections, why not call for a catch-up, or consider inviting everyone round for a meal? Taking time to regain

ANXIETY NO-NOS

Want to keep the worry down? Psychotherapist Terri Cole lists four things to avoid:

■ **Caffeine** – it's a stimulant, which means it gets your system working faster; if you're feeling anxious, you want to calm your system down instead.

■ **Dehydration** – lack of water interferes with the brain and body function, so we need plenty of fluids to stay healthy.

■ **Alcohol** – many of us could "use a drink" when we're nervous, but it also dehydrates us and can make us process oxygen less efficiently, which strains the system. Besides this, it's a temporary fix; long-term, we need better ways to tackle the problem.

■ **Lack of sleep** – rest is vital: the brain regenerates itself during sleep (see pp132–33).

Getting out of hand?

How stressed do you feel in general? There's a difference between a worried period and an anxiety disorder: the former passes, while the latter can become chronic if you don't address it. Consider taking a clinical questionnaire to help you determine whether it's something more serious – try searching for a "GAD-7 questionnaire" online. GAD (Generalized Anxiety Disorder) affects 6.8 million adults in North America alone.

The basic rule should be that anxiety, while always uncomfortable, should not dominate you. If it's starting to feel like it's undermining your quality of life, it's best to seek help from a medical professional.

Finding inner peace

Are you an old hippy or a lifelong rationalist? Either way, science suggests that meditation can be surprisingly effective. A study published in the *Journal of Personality and Social Psychology* tested meditation techniques on retirees to see what effects they would have on the participants' wellbeing and longevity. Those who practised meditation and mindfulness were shown to have increased odds of longer life, as well as improved cognitive function, blood pressure, and mental health. It seems that meditation really does make us healthier and happier.

ANXIETY QUICK FIXES

Combating anxiety may be a long-term project, as you adjust to your new life in retirement. If you've got a clinical anxiety issue you should seek professional help, otherwise there are a couple of things you can do to keep calmer until you feel more settled.

1 **Exercise** – do what's physically possible for you rather than over-straining yourself, but even moderate exercise releases endorphins, which calm the system down. Research suggests that people who exercise regularly are up to 25 per cent less likely to develop anxiety disorders.

2 **Human contact** – we're a social species, and being together is calming. A study at the University of North Carolina, for example, found that holding hands and hugging a loved one measurably lowered heart rate and blood pressure. Time with people you care about, especially if you can get soothing physical contact, may help keep you on an even keel.

control of your situation can go a long way to re-establishing your sense of calm and wellbeing.

TALKING IT OVER
HOW OTHER PEOPLE CAN HELP

We all know it can be good to talk things through. After you've retired, however, it can become all the more important – so how do you make sure you've got support well established in your life?

Leaving a work community can be a culture shock; the workplace will no longer be your primary social environment. This is the time to talk to loved ones: identifying yourself as a member of a supportive group of people can be a tremendous psychological safety net.

Don't want to be a burden?

If your main emotional resource is your children, you may feel a certain reluctance about changing roles: parents are used to looking after their kids, not the other way around. However, it can be useful to apply the concept of "social capital" to your situation. Coined by US psychologist Toni Antonucci, the idea is that in middle life, we tend to "invest" support in those around us – particularly children and younger friends – and in that period, we give more support than we get. However, as we get older and our younger relations and friends grow more independent, the situation reverses: we have "banked" credit with them, and they start to pay it back. The "emotional bank account" model only works if you are on good terms with your children, of course, but there's a fair chance they'll be more willing to be supportive than you think: people actually tend to feel more comfortable when there's a degree of balance in social exchanges.

At the same time, you don't have to give up your role as parent. As professor of Human Development Suzanna Smith points out, "giving is an enduring part of the parental role – parents continue to provide, as well as receive, support". Generally, we feel better about ourselves if we can still offer wisdom and encouragement to our children, but asking for emotional support doesn't preclude being a mum or dad figure.

Smaller and better

Of course, not all of us have children, or nieces and nephews, nor indeed an enormous circle

Q LEFT OUT IN THE COLD?

There's a common supposition that men aren't good at asking for help – but data suggests a slightly more complicated story. A 2007 study by US researchers asked retirees to fill in questionnaires on how much contact and support they had. The researchers found that, despite an initial hesitancy to seek help, men gradually caught up with women, and ended up with similar levels of support.

? WHAT TYPE OF SUPPORT DO YOU NEED?

British psychologist Derek Milne identifies four sub-categories of interpersonal support. When it comes to retirement, we'll probably need all of them at different times; in the early days, emotional support and companionship may be particularly valuable. If you're able to be clear with your loved ones which you need right now, it can help ensure that your needs are met during the transition.

Companionship: just being there.

Practical: helping out with tangible things.

Emotional: listening and caring.

Informational: helping us figure out what we need to know.

of friends to stand in for them. Is this a problem? Actually, retirees in general tend to have smaller social circles – which is no bad thing. Psychologist Laura Carstensen identifies our need for "socioemotional selectivity": we prune our networks more carefully when we feel that life is short and we don't have time to waste on people we don't really enjoy having around. In a study conducted with her colleague Frieder Lang, Carstensen concluded that older people tend to have fewer "friends" than younger people, but about the same number of close friends. We talk of the importance of a supportive network, but it doesn't have to be a *large* network: most retirees, in fact, prefer to focus on a handful of people they really trust – quality trumps quantity.

Beyond the family
For many people, children and grandchildren feature prominently in their support network, but non-relations can fill the same role just as well. For those of us without offspring, it's likely that we've invested more in our friends anyway; post-retirement, it's just a case of capitalizing on those connections that you've already made. As psychologist Mo Wang and sociologists Kène Henkens and Hanna van Solinge pointed out in a 2001 study, retirees' social resources can come from volunteer work or intermediary employment, as well as through their spouses; your options for socializing come from many different sources. As you start your retirement, look to all of your social environments, and start focusing on the people you really want to have around.

STRESS-MAPPING
STAYING ON TOP OF CHANGE

The transition to retirement can be a tricky period of adjustment. Keeping a log of any symptoms of stress can help you to cope. Some anxiety is normal – and in time will usually fade as you discover the positive.

A s a major life event, retirement can bring its stresses, often bound up with issues of undermined identity, loss of purpose and community, and health and money worries. To live a fulfilled life in retirement, you need to recognize these stresses and find ways of dealing with them. It helps to do this systematically by "stress-mapping" – a form of self-analysis that puts anxieties in context.

Often, when stress does gain inroads, the damage is caused by signs and symbols – especially the idea of leaving work as an ending to a worthwhile enterprise. The answer is to counteract the negative with positive images of equal strength, such as retirement as a new dawn – a chance to be independent, reinvent yourself, and fulfil ambitions. Psychologists recognize that we have an innate capacity to make the best of things – we are all remarkably resilient.

A TYPICAL STRESS PROFILE

Many people experience a rise in anxiety immediately after they leave work, followed by a gentle easing of stress levels. Try measuring your own stress levels each month using the "stress log" opposite.

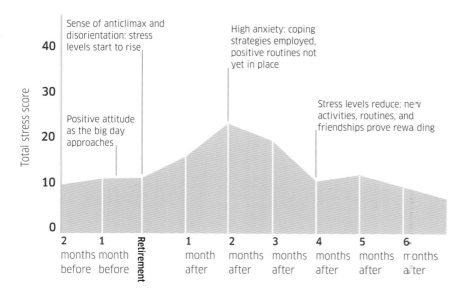

MEASURING YOUR STRESS PATTERNS

Yale University professor Rajita Sinha devised this self-assessment "stress log". Use it in the build-up to retirement and every month after the big day to see how stressed you have been during the preceding month. Enter numerical scores according to the key below, then add them up to find your total score.

Key
0 never
1 almost never
2 sometimes
3 fairly often
4 very often

Scoring: total up the scores. Higher scores denote greater stress, with a score of 20 or more indicating high levels of stress. Keep a log to compare your scores from month to month, or plot them on a graph, as shown opposite.

PERCEIVED STRESS

How often have you felt that you were unable to control the important things in your life? ☐

How often have you NOT felt confident about your ability to handle your personal problems? ☐

How often have you felt that things were NOT going your way? ☐

How often have you felt difficulties were piling up so high that you could not overcome them? ☐

PHYSICAL STRESS

How often have you found it difficult to talk clearly owing to fast, shallow breathing – especially on the subject of retirement? ☐

How often have you lain awake at night unable to sleep? ☐

How often have you had stomach cramps, headaches or feelings of muscular tension? ☐

How often have you felt an irresistible urge to smoke, drink, or consume comfort food? ☐

24%

UPS AND DOWNS

A study team in the USA plotted the responses of retired people over an 8-year period straddling the year 2000 – 24 per cent **reported feeling stress** at some point.

SILVER LININGS

There is a corresponding positive for every negative you might perceive about retirement. For example:

■ Loss of position, status, or power can also be seen as the **recovery of the independent self**.

■ Loss of work community can be seen as **more time with friends and family**.

■ Reduced income can be viewed as an **opportunity to find your non-material values**.

■ Loss of purpose can be a **chance to find new projects**.

■ A sense of rejection might also be an **escape from routine and burdensome tasks**.

Make your own list of "translations" – changing the way you verbalize your situation can have positive psychological effects.

FUTURE GROWTH
CULTIVATING A HEALTHY ATTITUDE

Compared with the past, the future can seem like a void, and we can all feel lost and insecure. This is a good time to explore two belief systems, or mindsets, that you may be bringing with you.

When you've had a setback in the past, how have you reacted? Have you decided that you must not be "good at" something, or that obviously there were some difficulties, but maybe if you approach it again with more preparation things will turn out better next time? This is the difference between what psychologist Carol Dweck calls the "fixed mindset" and the "growth mindset" – and it's not just a method of dealing with setbacks. A constructive mindset is concerned with doubts and challenges – which can make all the difference when it comes to dealing with an uncertain future.

The benefits of growth

The basic principle of the growth mindset is that our qualities, abilities, and talents aren't set in stone: instead, they're something we cultivate through effort. It sounds simple, but it can make a serious difference to our prospects in life. Dweck cites an example in which Hong Kong university students were offered the chance to join a free course to improve their English – a crucial skill in their economy. While students with a growth mindset jumped at the opportunity, those with a fixed mindset tended to turn it down: to their thinking, if they weren't "good at" learning languages, there was no point – even though the course was free,

WHAT ARE YOU THINKING?

Suppose you have a difficult day early in retirement: you've been planning to join a local activist group to promote better environmental policies in your area, but you went to your first meeting and nobody seemed very interested in what you had to say. What might the fixed mindset and growth mindset reflections look like? Not surprisingly, the person with the growth mindset stands a better chance of becoming a productive member of the team:

FIXED MINDSET:

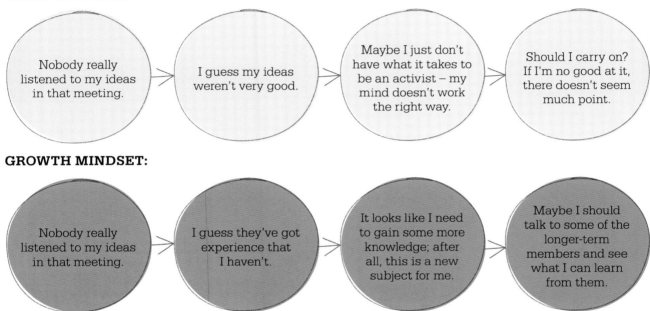

Nobody really listened to my ideas in that meeting.

I guess my ideas weren't very good.

Maybe I just don't have what it takes to be an activist – my mind doesn't work the right way.

Should I carry on? If I'm no good at it, there doesn't seem much point.

GROWTH MINDSET:

Nobody really listened to my ideas in that meeting.

I guess they've got experience that I haven't.

It looks like I need to gain some more knowledge; after all, this is a new subject for me.

Maybe I should talk to some of the longer-term members and see what I can learn from them.

meaning that they stood to lose nothing and could potentially gain a huge advantage in life.

Beyond self-consciousness

Nobody wants to make a fool of themselves, which means that if we expect failure at something, we're likely not to try. Dweck, however, reports that when tested to see how accurate they were at estimating their own abilities, it was people with a growth mindset who were "amazingly accurate". In many ways, it's a self-fulfilling

prophecy: you find out most about your abilities when you test them. Dweck asked people when they felt "smart": those with fixed mindsets said it was when they didn't make mistakes, whereas those with growth mindsets said it was when they were learning something new.

Retirement often means learning new things. The idea that "old dogs can't learn new tricks" is profoundly discouraging – but according to Dweck, it's also baffling with a growth mindset.

Q "PIG" OR "SET"?

Cognitive Behavioural Therapy uses the following two acronyms to describe our thought processes when we face setbacks:

Permanent: it will always be this way.
Internally created: it's caused by me.
General: this is just how the world is.

Specific: it went this way for a reason.
External: it's not personal.
Temporary: things may change.

So watch out for the "PIGs" and try to cultivate the "SET" explanations.

WHERE DO I FIT IN?

DEALING WITH ROLE CHANGE

We're more than our jobs, but psychologically speaking, the position we occupy in our various groups means a lot to us. When we retire those positions change, so how do we deal with that?

The psychological concept of "role theory" has been developing since the 1990s. The principle is this: we find our identity by occupying a set of roles. These can be both work- and non-work-related – but for most of us, the role our job created was an important part of our lives. The difficulty with retirement is that it's through these roles that we define ourselves both as individuals and as people connected to society. Retirement isn't just about letting go of a job, but about making a serious re-adjustment to your identity.

Finding new roles

When coming to terms with your new, post-retirement life, it's expecting too much of your psyche to shrug off an old role without feeling some discomfort; self-identity is a vital part of our psychological functioning. It's much more sustainable to identify new roles for yourself and start redefining yourself accordingly.

Is this harder if you really loved your old identity? Not necessarily: a US study from 2007 found that, surprisingly, how attached we are to our jobs isn't a strong predictor of how contented we are in retirement. In fact, people who identified with their jobs a lot are often happier retirees; research suggests that people who identify strongly with one role can find new roles and identify with them equally strongly.

SHARING THE LOAD

Good social relationships are crucial to managing role adjustments, but it's best not to rely too heavily on any single kind of relationship. Research suggests that there are four major styles of relationship retirees can draw on (see below). Each of them has its own benefits – you'll do best if you have a healthy mix.

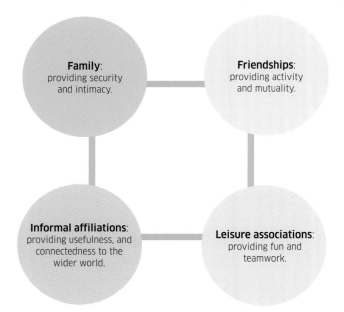

Family: providing security and intimacy.

Friendships: providing activity and mutuality.

Informal affiliations: providing usefulness, and connectedness to the wider world.

Leisure associations: providing fun and teamwork.

When looking around at your options, then, there are two important questions. First: what other roles – parent, friend, hobbyist, neighbour – do you already identify with? Second: what, if anything, did your job role give you that any of these other roles don't? The loss of a self-image can be more damaging than the loss of a specific role. If your job gave you a sense of leadership, for example, then the question might become: "Do any of my current other roles allow me to lead – and if not, where else can I turn to get that feeling?" It may be less a question of detaching from work than of re-attaching to something else: to detach comfortably from your job, your best bet may be to work on cultivating new roles outside it rather than lamenting the job itself. Redefining your identity in your own terms can be one of the most rewarding aspects of retired life.

Building confidence

For some of us, this transition is easier than others. According to psychologists Mary Anne Taylor-Carter and Kelli Cook, two qualities are particularly helpful for dealing with the work-retirement role transition: we need an "internal locus of control" (see pp146–47) –

 **ROLE WITH IT**

The university hospitals of Columbia and Cornell in the US recommend four ideas for managing role transitions:

1 **Be open to meeting new people** – being a friend is a powerful role.

2 **Play** – competitive games can keep us active, and exploratory "fooling around" can give us new ideas.

3 **Be creative** – we don't have to be great artists to get great benefits: even as an amateur, there's nothing like having the role of "musician" or "crafter" to be proud of.

4 **Pursue lifelong learning** – a new interest or area of expertise provides us with a fresh sense of self.

that is, we need to believe we have the power to shape our own outcomes; and we need "retirement self-efficacy" – the belief that we possess the necessary knowledge and skills to get by. The latter is likely to be bolstered by learning (see pp140–41); the former may be a long-term psychological project. The more you believe in your own power to adjust, the easier your adjustment is likely to be.

ALL CHANGE
RETIRING AND MOVING

Do you want a new home for your new life, or would you rather stay where you are? Retirees tend to have much more flexibility than working folk, so it may be time to consider your options.

As you start to settle into retirement, do you want to stay settled where you are, or might there be greener pastures elsewhere? A relocation can be the best or worst move you might ever make, so it's a decision to weigh up carefully.

Family and friends

If you're eyeing a new location speculatively, the big questions to ask yourself are:

- If you're in a relationship, does the new location meet both your and your partner's needs? If one of you is unhappy, the other probably will be too.
- Are you in reach of family and friends? A scenic place can pall if you're lonely, and as your

friends may have less energy to travel and your children may be busy, being too far removed can backfire. For them, travelling to you should be both manageable and affordable. You may want a bigger place to host family gatherings.

- Would you be leaving behind a social network or environment you love? Knowing your neighbours well can smooth over a lot of things. It isn't always easy to get a feel for a new place until you've actually lived there, so try renting for a while first (especially if you're relocating far from home).
- Do you have good or bad memories in your current home? How would you feel about leaving it all behind?

A great environment

You should also consider some practical issues about the area and the facilities that you need:

- Would you be happy there year-round? Mild winters can mean hot summers, and lively "summer towns" can shut down out of season: again, consider renting before you fully commit.
- Is there a chance of extreme weather such as flooding, storms, or earthquakes?
- What are the costs of living? Don't just factor in house prices, but property taxes, local rates, and the price of essentials such as food. It is particularly important to check if, or how, pensions are taxed locally.
- What are the costs of moving?
- Would it be easy to get part-time or volunteer work there if you wanted?
- Is everything you need in reach? A two-mile trek to the shops may be fine now, but you may

ON THE MOVE?

In the US, 64 per cent of retirees said they were likely to move at least once during their retirement. These are the most likely causes for doing so:

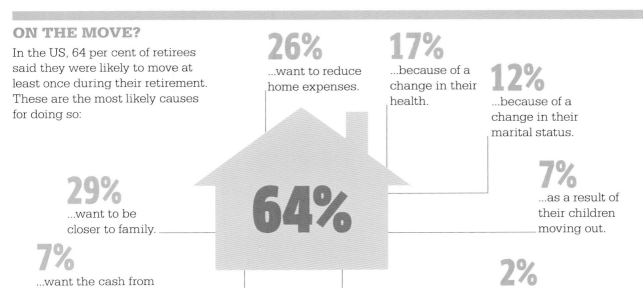

26% ...want to reduce home expenses.

17% ...because of a change in their health.

12% ...because of a change in their marital status.

7% ...as a result of their children moving out.

29% ...want to be closer to family.

7% ...want the cash from the sale of their home.

64%

2% ...for other reasons.

PROPERTY CHOICES

Of those who are already retired, 37 per cent have already moved. The choice of property for their new homes included:

51% ...moved somewhere smaller (usually to free up money and reduce maintenance).

30% ...moved somewhere larger (usually to make room for family).

37%

19% ...moved somewhere about the same size.

be less energetic in a decade's time. If you do have health problems, it is important to have easy access to decent medical facilities.

■ Do you have reliable professional contacts where you already are? For example, will you miss having a familiar car mechanic, accountant, solicitor, or hairdresser nearby?

■ Some places are specifically set up for seniors. On the positive side, they may have good facilities and other retirees around, but there may also be restrictions. Check all the rules.

Double trouble?

If you feel you might stretch to a second home to get the best of both worlds, what questions

should you ask then? Many are the same, but also consider:

■ How often could you visit? How will you maintain the property?

■ If you rent it out when you're not there, check what implications that will have on your taxable income.

■ Finally, is it well placed so you could host family get-togethers?

COPING SKILLS

LONG-TERM CHALLENGES

We'd all like to ensure that we have a trouble-free retirement, but it's a good idea to brace yourself for at least a few anxieties. The question is, how do we psychologically prepare for difficult situations?

Retirement will inevitably involve some bumps in the road: your own health may be more fragile than it used to be and your ability to bounce back from financial setbacks will probably be reduced. While you can make the best efforts in the world to plan sensibly, set up new goals and projects, and be part of a supportive community, life is uncertain and things can go wrong. We do best when we develop not just careful plans, but also a degree of resilience, so we can still cope should those careful plans go awry.

Who's in charge here?

Numerous studies have found that a key factor in coping well is having an "internal locus of control". The concept of "locus of control" is a technical way of describing where we attribute the power to change things. If we see ourselves as entirely subject

80%

HEALTH PROBLEMS?

If you're not in perfect health, you're not alone: 80 per cent of people over 65 in the US suffer from **at least one chronic condition**.

> With some exceptions, problem-focused **coping strategies**... lead to **positive health outcomes**.
>
> **Loriena Yancura, PhD and Carolyn Aldwin, PhD**

to fate or the whims of other people, our locus of control is outside of ourselves; on the other hand, if we consider ourselves to be capable of changing things through our own actions and efforts, that's an internal locus of control. This is more of a sliding scale than an either/or – we all vary in how empowered we feel – but research suggests that a high internal locus of control leads to better coping skills: we're more inclined to take positive action, and we're also likely to have more robust self-esteem.

A shift in perspective

It can be hard to break mental habits, of course, but cultivating the belief that you have at least some power over your own life can help. Try setting yourself some small, achievable projects, and as you get things done, make lists of how your own actions led to positive results. The more you remind yourself that you have at least some control, the easier it becomes to believe it.

When things do get out of our control, there's more than one way to meet the challenge

(see right). In adulthood we're generally required to use a lot of "problem-focused coping", but psychologists Loriena Yancura and Carolyn Aldwin point out this has its limits for retirees: some things, such as medical conditions and bereavement, can't be fixed. In those times, emotional and religious coping methods have been found to be more effective; other studies they cite suggest that "cognitive reframing" can reduce the stress of even serious diseases. People with a good ability to manage their feelings and adjust their attitudes have been found to feel better even under trying circumstances.

We can't control everything – although believing we can control at least some things is good for our wellbeing.

Q SEEING THE FUNNY SIDE

Counsellor David C. Borchard and minister Patricia A. Donohoe advise us in their book *The Joy of Retirement* to develop a "cosmic sense of humour". Classic dramatic comedies aren't free from disaster – ghastly things can happen to the characters. What is important, however, is that they traditionally end with the community coming together both reformed and transformed. The universe can throw bad things at us too, but if we can find ways to laugh – maybe not in the painful moment, but later when we've had some time to heal – it becomes easier to put ourselves back together.

Retirement is likely to involve some situations where you have to decide how much you can solve and how much you'll have to accept. Acceptance isn't the same as defeat, however: it's an active decision that involves genuine psychological competence.

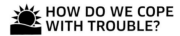 **HOW DO WE COPE WITH TROUBLE?**

In an overview of recent studies on how retirees manage stressful situations, psychologists Loriena Yancura and Carolyn Aldwin identify the following five methods of coping:

1 **Problem-focused coping**: trying to tackle the practical causes of a problem.

2 **Emotion-focused coping**: managing your feelings about a problem, such as trying not to dwell on it.

3 **Social support**: asking for sympathy and assistance.

4 **Religious coping**: seeking help from a higher power; praying for guidance or strength.

5 **Cognitive reframing**: or "meaning making" – trying to see the positive side of a problem, or reinterpreting the situation so it makes sense and feels tolerable.

ONLINE ASSISTANCE
HOW THE INTERNET CAN HELP

Welcome to your new friend the Internet. Today's retirement generation have spent most of their lives offline and can be a little wary, but if you approach it in the right way, you may be pleasantly surprised.

There's a so-called "grey divide" in Internet use: older people are more likely to be offline than on. However, older adults are also the fastest-growing group among Internet users, and there's no reason why you shouldn't join that cohort. It may be that you've grown used to dealing with the Internet in the course of your job, but if your experience is limited, does that mean you can't get value out of it now you're retired? Far from it: used wisely, the Net can become an outstanding resource.

What do I want from it?
The daunting thing about the Internet is that it's apparently infinite: finding anything you want may seem like needle-in-a-haystack territory, and getting the hang of the systems (how *do* you buy something from that shopping site anyway?) can take some practice. Navigating the Net is a bit like learning a language: once you grow fluent you can pretty much work things out as you go, but you need to be comfortable with it before you reach that point.

Where do I begin?
This is probably the time to find someone to guide you through things: fortunately, this is often fairly easy, as younger users tend to regard Internet usage as one of life's necessities and can be positively evangelical about

⑦ WHERE DO I START?

What do you actually want to do with the Internet? Communicate? Shop? Learn? Get involved with local groups? Here's a list of ideas to get you started:

1 **Keeping in touch** with friends and family. Email is a great resource, and social networking sites let you see the latest baby pictures and hear daily details of loved ones even when those loved ones are in other continents. If you can't watch your grandchildren grow up in the same town, you can still do it online.

2 **Following the news** and events. Most newspapers have websites now. If there's any breaking news, the Internet is likely to have rolling coverage that announces it first.

3 **Shopping**. From Christmas gifts to groceries, almost every business has an online shopping facility. If you're starting to feel too weary to haul home heavy bags, or if your local shops don't have what you want, the Internet can be a big help.

4 **Shared interest groups**. Gardener? Carpenter? Embroiderer? There will be Internet groups of like-minded souls, all keen to swap tips and share patterns and projects. Look out, too, for video tutorials: you can learn a whole new skill just from watching other people's demos, and there's a demo for practically everything.

5 **Community action**. Any campaign or improvement project will have an online mailing list, and probably an Internet petition as well.

6 **Reviews and guides**. If you're spending your retirement enjoying the good things in life, the Internet is the fastest way to find out whether critics recommend that new restaurant or play.

7 **Entertainment**. Movie and music streaming sites can give you more choice than your local video or record store ever did; there are sites that let you catch radio and TV shows you missed; the number of home-made videos people put up (some of which are pretty amusing) is nearly limitless.

8 **Family history**. If you feel retirement is a time to look back into your ancestry, genealogy is a billion-dollar industry online and one of the most popular reasons for using the Internet.

teaching. Consider the following when buying and obtaining advice on how to use a computer:

- Ask family and friends for recommendations about laptops, tablets, and desktop computers to find the most suitable one for you. Remember: touch-screen devices can be easier to use for anyone who has a problem typing or holding a mouse.
- When you buy a computer, don't succumb to sales patter. Start simply; you can always purchase more software as and when you feel you need it.

- If you don't know someone who can spare the time to teach you, check out local community groups, schools, and colleges for short courses devised especially for beginners.
- Whether you go on a course or get your grandchildren to teach you, don't be shy of asking even the most basic questions, such as "how do you switch the machine on in the first place?"

Pick your company

Here's a cautionary tale: in 2012 the social networking site Facebook (in collaboration with researchers from Cornell University in the US) performed a week-long secret experiment. For 689,003 users, they artificially slanted the emotional tone of posts that appeared in their feed: for some, positive-toned things were filtered out; for others, negative. The result? Those who got more cheerful things to read posted more positive things themselves, while the more negative posts had the opposite effect. What we were seeing was "emotional contagion": we tend to pick up the feelings of those we see around us – and that applies on the Internet too.

WHAT IS IT GOOD FOR?

A 2013 study published in the *Journal on Computing* asked senior citizens what they found most and least useful about using the Internet. Men and women gave very similar rankings – especially regarding what they didn't find helpful:

Group	Most useful	Least useful
Men	■ Communicating through chat rooms ■ Email ■ News and events	■ Playing online games ■ Monitoring bank accounts ■ Conducting investment transactions
Women	■ Watching videos ■ News and events ■ Listening to music and radio	■ Monitoring bank accounts ■ Conducting investment transactions
Men and women taken together	■ Watching videos ■ Listening to music radio ■ News and events	■ Playing online games ■ Monitoring bank accounts ■ Conducting investment transactions

This is fine if you're hanging out in nice places, but there's something to beware of: a 2013 study in Beijing found that the emotion that spreads fastest on the Internet – by a large margin – is anger. People share things that outrage them, they share people's hilarious rants about things that outrage them, they get dragged into "flame wars" (that is, furious arguments in which each side "flames", or berates, the other). And another study the same year found that while venting spleen on annoying people may feel cathartic at the time, in the long term, it doesn't help: the people who were angry on the Net were also angrier in general, and as its lead author Professor Ryan Martin commented, "people who vent end up being angrier down the road".

When all we see is someone's objectionable words on a screen it's tempting to view them as the embodiment of everything we can't stand, and retaliate. The science says: don't. Move along and find somewhere you like: nobody ever really wins an online argument. (A particular tip: be prudent about reading the comments on any news article or video. Silly people say silly things. It's probably better for your blood pressure to give them a miss.)

Be selective, ease yourself in, and be as clear as possible about what you'd most like to find – and the odds are, you'll find it and be glad you tried.

? WHAT'S THE PASSWORD?

To shop, to access certain things like films, and even to read some websites, you need a password. The search engine Google advises the following security tips:

1 Have a unique password for every important account. That way, if one is accessed, the others are still safe.

2 Store your list somewhere secure. Don't save passwords on your computer – if you're burgled or your computer is accessed, they'll be right there. If you keep a written list, don't leave it on your desk where anyone can find it.

3 Use a long password, and make sure it's hard to guess. "12345" or "password" are the first things a hacker will try; mix up letters and numbers, lower and upper-case characters, and refer it to something only you'll know, like "go2Gard3n2day" if you're a keen horticulturalist.

4 Keep your recovery options up-to-date. If you forget your password, you can get a reminder sent to an email account or your mobile phone, so make sure the reminders go to addresses and numbers you still use.

33%

TECHNICALLY FRIENDS

A 2014 study found that retirees were 33 per cent less likely to be depressed if they had a well-established **relationship with the Internet**. However, the study acknowledged that other studies didn't necessarily agree; a 2012 meta-analysis for Healthcare Informatics Research, for example, found that Internet usage didn't help clinical depression – but it did **reduce loneliness**. For retirees, it seems, often the best use of the Internet is to keep in touch with established friends and family: if you're far away, it can be a good way to get social support – and that, in turn, might make you feel less vulnerable to depression.

Q IDENTITY MATTERS

If you're a woman and you plan to join chat rooms or online games, choose a gender-neutral name. The Net contains a proportion of men who are online because nobody offline likes them, and a female username is more likely to draw sexual comments, harassment, and even stalking. So if you join an unfamiliar community on the Net, save yourself a headache and pick a different name.

OFF AND AWAY

TIME FOR A BIG VACATION?

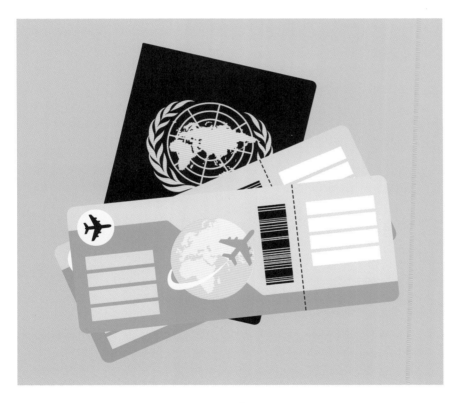

Retirement is an unmatched opportunity to go on that big adventure you've always planned, especially if you're still in good health. You've finally got as much time as you like, so why not see the world?

A holiday might be just what you need to celebrate the end of one era and the beginning of another. Striking out on the adventure of a lifetime, or simply sunbathing on a beach for a week or two, can be an important psychological marker of your transition from work to retirement – as well as being good fun.

Where to go?

How adventurous do you feel? Some of us yearn for the open road while others of us favour familiar turf. Your preferences may depend partly on where you're starting from: one study found that city-dwellers tended to travel further from home than people from the country. The ideal holiday destination is distant from our usual circuit but not completely outside our comfort zone, so be honest with yourself about how far is far enough and choose what will be the best fit for you.

Travelling companions

If you're able to travel with your partner, this could be the opportunity for a second honeymoon. Travelling with friends can also be a good option, but may be tricky timing-wise unless you retire around the same time. If you want to go it alone but need some outside support, group tours may be the solution; they also spare you the hassle of booking and planning. Physical limitations need not prevent you from participating in active tours; tour guides are well accustomed to dealing with the differing needs of senior travellers, and can adjust activities for varying mobility and energy levels.

When shall I go?

Take advantage of the "shoulder season" (usually April–May and September–October), when the weather is clement in many regions, the crowds are thin, and flights and accommodation are significantly cheaper. Make the most of your freedom, and stay abroad for as long as you like.

Q TRAVEL SMART

Consider these tips for older travellers when planning your next adventure:

- Pack a magnifying glass and small torch for reading fine print and poring over detailed maps.
- Bring a notebook to jot down reminders.
- Keep any medications in labelled containers and store them in your hand luggage.
- Check for upper age limits on car rentals before you settle on a destination.
- Ask about senior discounts everywhere you go.

GREAT ESCAPES

What motivates us to travel, and what do we want when we go abroad? A 2008 Israeli study interviewed retired travellers and found five key themes:

1 **Retirement as opportunity** – fewer obligations means more freedom, so seniors often see retirement as a new horizon.

2 **Finding breaks to suit your needs** – health, money, and responsibilities back at home can limit your holiday options. Shorter breaks or action-packed holidays can help you negotiate these contraints.

3 **Spillover between leisure and tourism** – retirees often travel to pursue their particular hobbies; travel planning can also become a hobby in itself.

4 **Travelling may preserve old interests** – while travel may be seen as a chance to learn new things, retirees often see it as a way to pursue previous work- and non-work-related interests too.

5 **Travelling is for quality times with loved ones** – family and friends are regularly cited as retirees' prime motivation for travelling (see left).

IS HOME WHERE THE HEART IS?

Travel can be a great way to stay connected with loved ones. A 2008 study found three key ways to involve them in your travel plans:

Taking joint trips with children and grandchildren.

Travelling to **visit friends and family** in other parts of the world.

Renting or buying a holiday home and **inviting loved ones to stay**.

CHAPTER 5
LIVING WELL

LOOKING AFTER YOU AND YOURS

IN THE MIRROR
SAFEGUARDING YOUR HEALTH

All of us would like to stay fit and well in retirement. Once you've taken control of your schedule, how do you incorporate taking care of your health into your new lifestyle?

If you've got your health, your retirement will be a lot more comfortable – and it's good to be aware of both physical and mental health. We can't stop ourselves from aging or getting certain conditions, but keeping a baseline of wellbeing can make those things a lot easier to manage.

Hitting the gym

There are good ways to get mild exercise, such as walking and cycling instead of driving, swimming, dance classes, running around after grandchildren – even gardening or doing the chores vigorously can work up a good sweat – but it can be rewarding to tackle something more intensive. When you think of the gym, do you picture a friendly place, or an intimidating room full of muscular twenty-somethings sneering from the treadmills?

If it's the latter, you may be in luck: a lot of gyms have woken up to the fact that health-conscious retirees are worth cultivating. It makes financial sense: retirees have plenty of time to work out and are likely to be concerned about their health, and as such are a valuable market. Look out for gyms that have senior programmes: some run sessions at quieter times of day such as 9–11am and 2–4pm – this is one of those ways you can take advantage of being free during working hours – and at those times they may also turn down the pounding music and even organize group sessions.

Nobody wants to feel hopelessly outclassed by their juniors, but many gyms are starting to respect this, so watch out for places that specifically cater to you – you may find more than you expect.

Getting your check-ups

If you have any chronic health issues you need to keep an eye on them, but even if you don't, regular visits to the doctor are a good plan. It's also worth scheduling mental health check-ups: as *Psychiatric News* editor Jeffrey Borenstein puts it, "It's just as important as having a physical check-up." Doctors have standard sets of questions they use to check for common issues such as depression and anxiety, so ask about those as well as getting your blood pressure tested. Some symptoms are easy to mistake for just "being retired" or "getting older" – and if they're actually signs of mood disorders, you don't have to resign yourself to living with them.

Q STAYING LIVELY

Physical, mental, and social activity all contribute to our wellbeing. Peter Spiers, vice-president of not-for-profit organization Road Scholar, collaborated with a psychology professor from Brandeis University to survey over-55s. They classified their interviewees into five groups:

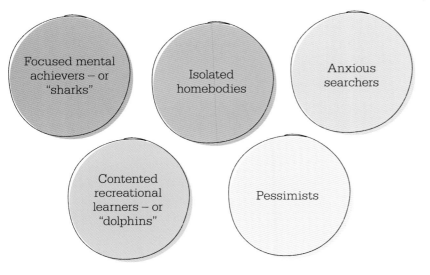

Of these, the happiest were what they called the "sharks and dolphins of retirement". They formed about half of the average population, and a higher proportion of the people on Spiers's programme.

What did these people have in common? They were pursuing interests – gardening, arts and crafts, exercise, volunteering, music, and educational travel were popular choices – that were rich in at least two of the following:

Socializing	**Moving**	**Creating**
Keeping in touch with friends and family, and getting out and meeting new people.	This means formal "exercise", but also activities that naturally involved being physically active such as gardening or walking from place to place.	Not just art and writing, but crafts, learning a new instrument, and anything that challenged their more inventive and perceptive side.

Our sense of wellbeing is partly physical and partly mental, but the brain is a part of the body, so keeping both mind and body healthy is mutually beneficial.

GOOD HABITS?

It can be hard to live healthily when we're stressed at work; once we retire, the **greater flexibility** we experience seems to **help us keep our resolutions**. According to data analysis of 26,000 people over 50 in the US in 2014:

69%

...of those who ever reported smoking were still smoking shortly before retirement, while only...

56%

...were still smoking shortly after retirement.

48%

...of those still working exercised regularly, while...

52%

...of those who had been retired for several years exercised regularly.

It's worth noting that those who improved their habits most were those who'd *chosen* retirement: a sense of control over our fate (see pp146–47) tends to make us more proactive in other areas of life.

RETIREMENT BENEFITS

A 2014 report in *The Journal of Human Resources* noted that "results indicate that the retirement effect on health is beneficial and significant".

BRAVE NEW WORLD

HOW TECHNOLOGY CAN HELP

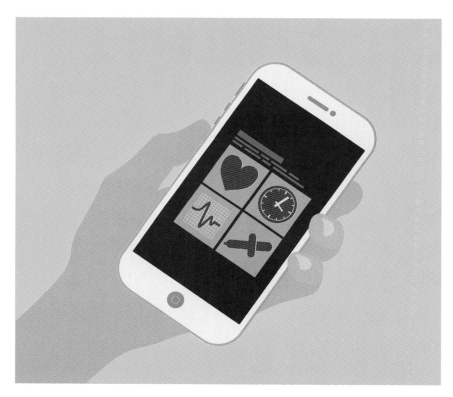

Are you mechanically minded, or would you rather leave technology alone? If you're facing health problems, certain kinds of technology might actually be the foundation of a safer and freer way of life.

I f you start to feel your age a bit, there's a good chance you'll be worried. Few of us are happy at the idea of losing our independence: the idea of staying free in our own homes for as long as possible is what most of us would prefer. If that sounds like you, it might be a weight off your mind to know that there are devices to help maintain your independence.

Equally, you might be healthy yourself but responsible for someone who isn't; many retirees have to take on caring responsibilities (see pp178–79), so wouldn't it make life easier if there was something to help you out?

If you need a helping hand, recent technology might actually turn out to be your best friend. It's increasingly easy to keep track of your health, and even call for help in a crisis, without needing full-time care. If you feel like you can mostly manage for yourself but have some physical issues that might cause you problems, some high-tech devices could improve your life for years to come.

What's the deal?

The term for these useful devices is "assistive technology", which consists of "telehealth" and "telecare" systems.

Telehealth systems use sensors installed in the home to monitor physical changes in your body, and if something does change, the sensors will pick it up. The

LIFE-SAVING TECH?

A study of several thousand people was performed by the UK Department of Health. For individuals whose homes were set up with "**telehealth**" (health monitoring technology) and "**telecare**" (alarm systems), the results were impressive:

45%

...reduction in mortality rates.

20%

...reduction in emergency admissions.

15%

...reduction in visits to Accident and Emergency.

information is relayed to a database monitored by somebody trained in the area, and if it looks as if something's going wrong for you, the information is sent to your doctor, who can revise your healthcare plan accordingly. Telecare systems are also sensor-based, but act as more of an alarm: if you trigger it, an alert goes out to summon help.

This may sound too intrusive – you may not want to be monitored that closely – but if you need help, technology could be the answer.

GREAT DEVICES

There are some excellent gadgets available to support retirees who need help around the house or who want peace of mind if they prefer to stay in their own homes. Recommendations from friends are always a good starting point, but you can also speak to health professionals, who will have up-to-date information about new technology.

"Telehealth" and "telecare" devices

You can install sensors and equipment in your house that call for help if something goes wrong. Telehealth sensors will monitor changes in blood pressure, oxygen levels, and body weight, and are useful for anyone suffering from long-term conditions such as chronic heart failure, diabetes, chronic obstructive pulmonary disease, and epilepsy.

Fall alarms

These are worn around the neck so they're with you throughout the day. Old radio-based systems tended to confine people to the home, but now you can get mobile phones with a built-in fall detector and alarm system that you can take with you anywhere.

Robotic vacuum cleaners

If your joints aren't as good as they used to be, a gadget that trundles around vacuuming for you could be a blessing.

Medication apps

You can get pillboxes that not only store your pills, but send you texts, emails or sound alerts to remind you when to take them.

Footwear with GPS tracking

If you're caring for someone with Alzheimer's, you'll know they can wander and get lost. There are now shoes available that send automatic alerts and help you track them to within 10m (30ft).

KEEPING YOUR EQUILIBRIUM

HOW TO AVOID OVERLOAD

An "active retirement" sounds so impressive – but do we have to overdo it? While none of us wants to feel bored and useless, sociologists suggest that it's also possible to put too much value on being busy.

In many books on retirement – including, on many pages, this one – you'll encounter a lot of recommendations for keeping yourself active. New employment, volunteering, hobbies, travel, socializing: all these are good things... but it's possible to have too much of a good thing. If you're feeling like you don't really want to treat retirement as a new, hectic job, there's a classic theory of gerontology known as the "busy ethic" that may ring a bell for you.

The busy ethic

Since the 1950s, researchers have been insisting that later life can be a lively and creative period. With better healthcare resulting in greater longevity, sometimes it can seem as though retirement is surrounded with the same exhortations to be productive as actual paid work.

> Retirement is **morally managed** and legitimated... in part by an ethic that **esteems leisure** that is earnest, occupied and **filled with activity**.
>
> **David Ekerdt**
> Sociologist

Q WHO PROMOTES THE BUSY ETHIC?

Sociologist David Ekerdt identifies three "parties to the busy ethic". None of this means that you should avoid activities, of course, but if others are making you feel under pressure to keep busy, at least this perspective allows you to understand what is happening.

Institutions
Those who sell and market services to seniors have a financial interest in keeping you shopping, and selling ways to keep you "active" is a great way to keep their businesses ticking over.

Retirees themselves
When "called upon to account for their lives", as Ekerdt puts it, "busy ethic" retirees are the people most likely to talk about how much they have to do, sometimes to the point where the busyness itself is more important than what they're actually doing.

Friends, relations and co-workers
Some people are keen to chat about about what you're "doing" once you have retired and like to assure you that it's great to keep busy. Those are your "busy ethic" friends and family members – who often subconsciously want to be reassured that, yes, there is life after work.

This is what sociologist David Ekerdt calls the "busy ethic". The idea is a fairly simple one: when a culture starts to value certain qualities, we don't necessarily re-evaluate these qualities when it comes to retirees and how they live their lives. In practice, if leisure is as high-pressured as a job, it risks taking the fun out of it.

What's the point?
Why do we cling to this "busy ethic"? Ekerdt identified four main motivations:

- **It legitimizes leisure**. We're not usually comfortable with "idle" people: with the busy ethic, you're still "busy", even if you're not technically working.
- **It symbolically defends** you against aging. If you're active, you're still considered youthful.
- **It lets you have "time off"**. By creating regular habits of activity, you can still take "holidays" from your pursuits without feeling guilty.
- **It "domesticates"** retirement in line with mainstream values. A shamelessly inactive retiree,

many fear, might set a bad example. It tells the younger generations that busyness is all there is in life.

If all this sounds moralistic (not to mention stressful for older retirees), that's because it is. There's nothing wrong with keeping yourself occupied – boredom is good for no one – but don't let yourself feel obligated. Staying busy just for the sake of it is a cultural compromise that you don't need to make unless you choose to.

TIME TOGETHER

DEALING WITH RELATIONSHIP CHANGE

Once you're both at home it might be a great romance – finally, you're together as much as you choose – but it could also turn into a subtle turf war. How do you keep love alive while still keeping the peace?

Many of us long to have more time together when we're stuck at work, but once you are together for long periods, your fondness may hit some rocky patches. Little irritants can magnify; imbalances in your roles at home can be thrown into sharp relief; areas in which you don't have much in common become more important. The transition to being a retired couple can be one of those times when you have to work on your relationship.

Good news and bad

Realistically, the early days of retirement can be hard on both of you. A 2001 study by researchers at Cornell University in the US found that both men and women reported the "highest marital conflict" and "lowest marital satisfaction" just after they'd stopped work. But it also found that those who'd been retired for two or more years were the happiest couples of all. So how do you achieve that?

It's good to talk

Retirement experts Rob Pascale and Dr Louis H. Primavera advise that you include your expectations for each other when discussing your retirement plans. For example, if you don't want unasked-for advice about cooking the dinner or you want the shed to remain your own domain, speak now; if you decide to share household chores,

SEVEN STEPS TO A HAPPY RELATIONSHIP IN RETIREMENT

After interviewing several hundred subjects, writer and consultant Miriam Goodman identified seven recommendations for a happy relationship in retirement. Consider each step by yourself, and then with your partner. It can also pay to revisit these steps once in a while if you feel that something you agreed on previously has not turned out as you would have wished.

1
Take your time
You don't have to do everything you planned together right away, so be patient with each other as you both adjust.

4
Share responsibilities
Once you're both home, fair is fair, and unequal workloads around the home can cause resentment.

3
Stay connected
Connecting with the "outside world" – for example through friendships, volunteering, and clubs – can give you a bit of breathing space.

2
Speak up
If your partner wants something you don't, let them know. You'll have less time away from each other now, so don't let suppressions turn into grudges.

5
Stay active together
Your exercise plans will be much easier to stick to with a companion, and it gives you a shared interest.

6
Take time out
Schedule in some time when you can both be alone.

7
Make plans
Schedule some time to relax or do activities together, but avoid the temptation to do *too* much.

say so, but let the person taking on new jobs choose which ones they want so they feel more involved.

Most of us want to feel close to our partners, but we probably feel best if we can co-exist without having to "merge" entirely. The psychologist Maryanne Vandervelde suggests that we remember the secret of "parallel play": the comfort of being near one another as you pursue independent interests can be one of the greatest pleasures we experience. Staying close but not being co-dependent is a lifelong challenge in relationships, and retirement brings its own tests. If you can manage it, however, you might just get the best of both worlds.

A WORKING PARTNER?

ADJUSTING TO DIFFERENCE

Not every couple lives in absolute synchrony. Whatever the reason, the odds are good there'll be a period – perhaps only of months, perhaps of years – when only one of you is retired. What then?

When you're part of a couple, lots of things can lead to different retirement times. Perhaps there's an age gap that means one of you is approaching retirement sooner; perhaps you aren't ready to give up both incomes yet; perhaps one of you is facing redundancy or health problems; perhaps one of you still feels more career energy than the other. (Especially if a woman has taken time out to care for children: once she gets back to work, she may prefer to stay on for longer.) Whatever your reasons, it's a common issue to tackle.

Keeping in sync

On the whole, we prefer to retire fairly close, time-wise, to our partners – in fact, this tends to influence us more than our age. If your partner is younger than you, there's a likelihood that you may want to stay employed for longer – though be sure you aren't taxing yourself beyond your physical and mental strength to do so.

Managing money

Few marital conflicts are nastier than the ones about money, but when one of you is still working and the other's retired, you can face friction even if the working partner is decent enough not to use their income as leverage for more power in the home. (In fact, you really mustn't do this – and conversely, the retired person should make sure not to falsely accuse their partner of doing this to win a conflict. Using money as a reason for fighting dirty is never a good idea.) The problem is simply that it may be hard for a still-earning partner, who hasn't directly experienced life with no pay packet at the end of the month, to see the retired partner's point of view. This is a situation where going to a financial adviser together (see pp100–01) is probably the best solution: impartial advice can help keep money conversations from getting too personal.

Managing attention

When one of you is still working, there can be a temptation to feel that one of you is still "having a life" while the other isn't. The retired spouse can feel bored, depressed, or under-valued – especially if there's the sense that it's their job to do all the housekeeping to make themselves "useful" – while the working spouse can feel under pressure to leave work early to get home – which only creates job stresses and possible resentments. Living two very different lives can put a strain on both of you.

What's the solution? If one of you has retired because of health reasons, the other may eventually need to consider taking on carer responsibilities or else finding a temporary carer (see pp178–79) – but if the retired spouse is still relatively active and well,

KEEPING COMPANY

According to a 2008 survey for AARP (formerly the American Association of Retired Persons), the majority of retirees would encourage their partners to join them. It seems we may come across as more gentle in our encouragements than we think, but most of us would like company in our retirement.

Of those who were asked how strongly their retired partners had encouraged them to retire too:

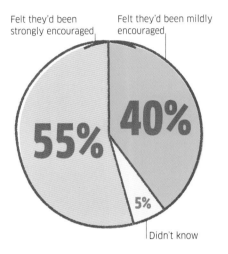

Felt they'd been strongly encouraged

Felt they'd been mildly encouraged

55%
40%
5%

Didn't know

Of those retired respondents who were asked how strongly they encouraged their partners to retire:

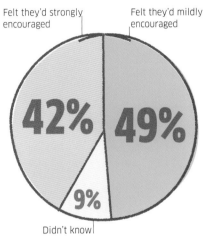

Felt they'd strongly encouraged

Felt they'd mildly encouraged

42%
49%
9%

Didn't know

developing interests and activities of their own is likely to be key (and even if there are some health limits, a lot can be done from the home if you get involved online – see pp148–51).

This may sound like you are being palmed off, but actually it is contributing something substantial, because it means being a trailblazer who can then give their partner the benefit of their experience when the second retirement finally happens: the more the working spouse can appreciate their partner's experiments, the more positive both of you are likely to feel.

less than
20%

RETIRE TOGETHER

According to a 2013 study by the Center for Retirement Research at Boston College, fewer than 20 per cent of couples **retire in the same year**.

ONLY CONNECT
SEX AND COMPANIONSHIP

We have a psychological need to feel close to our partners, and physical connection forms an important part of this intimacy. Retirement can be a great opportunity to build on your connection.

When we're not as young as we used to be, sex isn't always straightforward: we may feel we're losing interest, or still have the interest but not quite the capacity we once had – or else find that our partner has different needs. Reduced libido or compromised physical capacity can have a negative impact on your wellbeing, but there are plenty of strategies you can use to ensure that you continue to have a fulfilling sex life.

Numerous studies have found that "conjugal satisfaction" is strongly associated with better health and happiness in retirement – and since you and your partner will have a lot of days together, creating a rewarding physical relationship is something you'll have plenty of time to enjoy.

Q WITHOUT YOU

It's easy to talk of sex while your partner is there and willing, but suppose you make sex central to your lives and then one of you can no longer manage?

A 2003 study at the University of Sheffield found that couples in this situation tended to decrease the importance they placed on sex, starting to frame it to themselves as a natural consequence of aging. If you or your partner aren't quite capable of "full" sex, don't lose out on physical closeness altogether: you can still be intimate without sex (see p169).

60%

BETTER TOGETHER

A 1989 study found that 60 per cent of heterosexual married couples said their **sex life had improved** since the husband's retirement.

Losing potency?

There's a common belief that men peak sexually in their teens, and then it's all downhill from there. In fact, research suggests that while older men may need more time to warm up and feel sensations less intensely, they also tend to feel those sensations in a more sensual and diffuse way, and may be able to control their performance better – all of which makes it easier to satisfy and feel emotionally close to a partner.

For a man whose potency really has suffered as he's aged – about one in seven men get prostate cancer at some point, for example, and the attendant surgery can have unwanted consequences – it's always worth putting your embarrassment to one side and talking to a doctor. This can be an uncomfortable topic for some, so be aware that you can specify the gender of your doctor if this makes it easier for you. Doctors

UNREALISTIC EXPECTATIONS

While our levels of self-esteem have a big impact on our sex lives (see pp168–69), so too can our expectations of our partners. A 2008 study in Montreal interviewed retirees about their sexual activity, and identified a number of assumptions that tended to make things difficult for both parties:

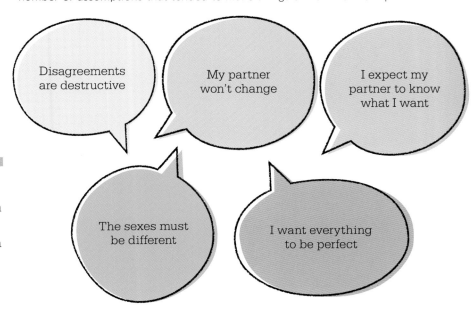

In reality, being able to talk things through is the foundation of a good sex life, not a sign that something's wrong. The more relaxed we feel, the better off we are. The researchers worked on improving communication, sex education (including exercises to increase sensual awareness, explore fantasies, and improve understanding), and teaching "cognitive reframing" (see pp146–47) – that is, learning to look at things in new ways – among the couples. While the results didn't much affect the participants' levels of sexual desire, the couples did consistently feel more satisfied with the sexual relationship they already had. Open communication seems to be the key to a happy sexual partnership.

remark that since Viagra came out in 1998, men tend to find it easier to ask for help: naming the drug you want rather than the symptom you have can feel less personal. (Although it's worth noting that there are actually a variety of drugs available; Viagra is just the most well-known brand name.) However, physical functioning is only part of the picture. A study published in the *International Journal of Impotence Research* found that medication is more effective if coupled with better understanding of how sexual responses change with age. Whatever your circumstances, some later-life sex education is undoubtedly a good idea.

»

›› Beyond "the change"

About 75 per cent of women experience at least some symptoms with menopause, but whether it means your sex life has to diminish is another question. The trouble with current studies is that they tend to focus on women who are having problems, which means that problems tend to be over-represented when people write about sex and post-menopausal women. What research we have suggests that older women may need longer foreplay and gentler intercourse, and may particularly benefit from using a commercial lubricant, but with these in mind, there's no reason that a retired woman should have to stop enjoying herself.

One thing to be aware of is the effect of hysterectomy: about 30–40 per cent of women in the US have one during their lifetimes, and it can have unforeseen effects. Particularly problematic is the fact that the clitoris has been an under-appreciated organ for a long time. Before urologist Helen O'Connell of the Royal Melbourne University published her findings in 1998, demonstrating that the clitoris involved a great deal more internal nerves than previously supposed, doctors performing hysterectomies didn't have the full information about which nerves to carefully avoid. If you've had a hysterectomy, the effects on your pleasure can be complicated – for some women it's better, for some it's worse, and for some it's just different. If you're really not feeling what you used to pre-surgery, don't suffer in silence – discuss your options with your doctor.

All in the mind?

A great deal of sex and intimacy is more about our attitudes than anything physical. Expectation plays a big part: we're all influenced by society's ideas of what people like us "do" and "don't do"; research suggests that in societies that, for example, expect men to remain sexually active all their lives, men do indeed tend to remain sexually active. Meanwhile, women are particularly vulnerable to the notion that older people are unattractive and that unattractive people aren't "sexy" – a sad and pointless conclusion if you're still eager to enjoy yourself. There is no age limit for sex, and most people continue to enjoy what they've always enjoyed. Doing our best to shake off stereotypes and focus on what we personally want rather than what we're supposed to do is an excellent first step towards a more fulfilling love life.

WHO'S DOING IT?

A 2015 study at Manchester University found that:

54%
...of men over 70 were sexually active and

31%
...of women over 70 were sexually active.

Of these, a third reported they were having **"frequent"** sex – which the researchers classed as at least twice a month.

Q UNDERSTANDING OBSTACLES

Fear often holds us back from achieving happiness; consider whether your anxieties are effecting your enjoyment of sex:

- **Emotional baggage** – psychological stresses, such as anxiety and depression, can affect your libido and your ability to connect with your partner.

- **Negative body image** – if you're too busy worrying about wrinkles or love handles, you're probably not having a good time!

- **Low self-esteem** – big life changes can affect your sense of identity in a negative way, which can make you feel less attractive.

- **Worries about "performance"** – worrying about how you will "perform" or whether your sexual partner will find you attractive can prevent arousal in both sexes.

JUST GOOD FUN?

We all know that sex can be fun, but what else is it good for? Studies suggest that fun between the sheets can have positive and wide-ranging effects on other areas of your life, too:

IMPROVING YOUR HEALTH

Sex can be good exercise; arousal increases your heart rate, which reaches its peak during orgasm. Increased frequency of sex as we age is also associated with physical benefits to both men and women's sexual organs.

RELEASING "FEEL-GOOD" ENDORPHINS

Sexual activity causes the brain to release endorphins, giving you a natural high.

SOLIDIFYING YOUR RELATIONSHIP

A fulfilling sexual relationship strengthens your bond with your partner.

 ## FINDING INTIMACY

It's easy to forget that physical closeness doesn't have to mean actual intercourse. Much of what's rewarding about sex is simply being close, and that's possible no matter what the state of your health is. If you want to try some new ways to feel intimate, give some of these ideas a try:

■ Long embraces with romantic music playing.

■ Stroking each others' skin with different textures (such as feathers, fur, and silk).

■ Long, unbroken eye contact.

■ Giving each other massages.

■ "Grooming" each other: brush each others' hair, wash each others' skin, play together with scented soaps and lotions.

■ Writing and reading each other love letters.

We talk about "lovemaking", and while sex is a great pleasure, love is what we need the most. You may be feeling limber and tiger-ish when you climb into bed, but if you're not, don't close the book on your physical relationship. In the end, it's about enjoying being together, and whatever makes you happiest is what's right for you.

Q OLDER AND WISER

Follow these tips to help you make the most of your sex life:

✔ **Celebrate your experience** – we're often more body-confident when we're older than when we were twenty-something. Independence and self-confidence are sexy.

✔ **Look ahead** – we inevitably change as we age, so avoid comparing your sex life now to when you were younger.

✔ **Appreciate yourself** – accept the natural changes that come with age, and don't let grey hair or wrinkles stop you enjoying your own body.

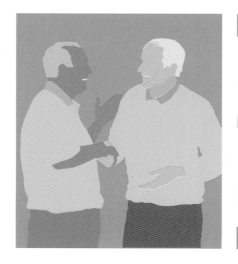

GETTING TOGETHER
WHO ARE YOUR TRUE FRIENDS?

When you're free to set your own schedule, who do you want to spend your days with, and why? Now is the time to seek out kindred spirits, and to invest energy in friendships old and new.

Whether old-established or new-found, friends make all of our lives richer. You don't have to spend every minute of the day with your buddies – some research suggests, in fact, that the amount of time we spend with them increases only slightly once we're retired – but whether you're chatting for hours or just taking comfort in the knowledge that they're there if you need them, the platonic relationships in your life are well worth the energy they take to maintain.

What makes a good friend?

Studies have consistently found that when describing an ideal friend, everyone from childhood to old age paints the same picture: the key qualities are always, as psychologists Willard Hartup and Nan Stevens put it, "mutuality... social giving and taking, and returning in kind or degree". We value people who give us a two-way relationship – not those who take advantage or shower us with unwanted favours, but rather those who reciprocate and share.

It's a particularly good idea to cultivate the friends whose influence you appreciate. Recent studies by researchers Nicholas Christakis and James Fowler have found that there's an element of "contagion" in our social relationships: if an individual smokes or is overweight, or is cooperative or happy, then the odds are higher that their friends and friends-of-friends will be too. Of course, this doesn't mean you should ostracize everyone who likes the odd cigarette or could lose a few pounds, but it does mean that we should cultivate the friendships that draw out the sides of ourselves that make us happiest.

Growing together

If you have other retired friends, how do you feel about each others' interests? Adult education courses are a great way to make new friends with similar interests. However, mature students can

🔍 TAKING IT EASY

While marriages can develop more friction over time, a 2009 US study found that the reverse is true of our relationships with our friends: as we age and mellow, our friendships grow more warm and tolerant.

CHATTING ONLINE

Fond of social media? A Pew Research Center project in 2013 found that the number of Facebook "friends" we have gets smaller with each generation. However, it's worth noting that younger generations are less likely to have met all of their Facebook friends, or to be particularly close to many of them; if you have 50 people in your life whom you genuinely like, that's plenty.

Median number of Facebook friends:

Older generations
(born before 1955)

50

Younger baby boomers
(born 1956–1964)

98

Generation X
(born 1965–1980)

200

Millennials
(born after 1981)

250

often find themselves drifting apart from old connections: learning new things and developing new opinions can distance you from people who have a vested interest in you staying the same person. If you are eager to expand your mind, it might be a good idea to find other retired friends to join you in your class: it's more sociable, and if you do find your preoccupations changing, your valued friends will be changing right along with you. Look for others who, like you, want to continue to broaden their horizons after retirement.

Quality vs quantity

Statistically, the number of friendships we have in retirement tends to be lower than it was before, but that doesn't need to matter – it's the casual friendships that tend to drop away. A 1997 French study found that, while it's helpful to have a good number of relationships, the really important factor is quality. Subjects with the most affectionate and supportive relationships were found to be both physically and mentally healthier, and even more long-lived. So seek out your friends and get ready to age happily together.

? WHERE CAN YOU MEET NEW PEOPLE?

If you're looking to expand your social circle, where do you start? Here are a few popular places for retirees to meet new friends:

- Health clubs and exercise classes
- Adult education courses
- Groups organized at the local library or senior centre
- Civic groups looking for volunteers
- Hobby clubs
- Hiking groups
- Alumni groups
- Card-playing groups
- Dog-walking or -training clubs
- Travel clubs
- Support groups

Don't forget: if your local area doesn't have the club you're looking for, you can always start one yourself.

FAMILY FAVOURS

LATE REWARDS OF PARENTHOOD

Your children have grown up, flown the nest, and are living lives of their own. Now that you can no longer exercise straightforward parental authority, how do you form a mutually supportive relationship?

There are great pleasures to be had from contemplating the fact that homework, university applications, and conflicts over curfews are all behind you. However, the relationship between parents and adult children may be complicated in new ways: it can be difficult to see your "baby" as a grown-up, and your child may now have their own ways of doing things that you don't like, but no longer have any control over. The ideal for child-parent relationships during retirement should be mutual affection, respect, and – on occasion – forbearance.

Don't take that tone with me
Children are family, and families – inevitably – fight. What's the best way to reduce conflict? One solution might be to identify exactly what's creating the strain. According to a study by the Gerontological Society of America,

more than 1/3

GIVE A HELPING HAND
A 2014 survey in the USA found that more than a third of parents of "millennials" provide at least some **financial support** to their children.

parents and adult children may have quite different ideas about what lies at the bottom of their disagreements. The study identified six major themes:

- Politics, religion, and beliefs.
- Standards of housekeeping and home maintenance.
- Habits and lifestyle choices.
- Communication and interaction style.
- Child-rearing practices and values.
- Work habits and attitudes.

Interestingly, the parents' biggest gripe was clashes over habits and lifestyle choices, whereas the children were more concerned about communication (see graph, right). Some subjects are just touchy – politics over the dinner table or criticizing someone's parenting are likely to start a quarrel with anyone – but if you feel there's more conflict than there needs to be, the solution might be easier than you think. Try having an open discussion with your child about what he or she is really objecting to – neither of your opinions are likely to change, but if your communication styles are the real problem, that's something you can both work on changing.

What keeps us together?

According to a study by US-based psychologists Vern Bengston and Robert Roberts, there are six key elements to family bonding:

KEEPING THE PEACE

The Gerontological Society of America found that parents and children had mildly differing ideas about what caused the most intergenerational conflict.

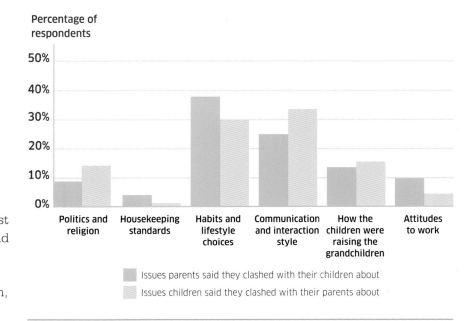

Percentage of respondents

Issues parents said they clashed with their children about
Issues children said they clashed with their parents about

- **Affection** – how warmly we feel and speak about each other.
- **Association** – how often we seek out each others' company.
- **Consensus** – how much we share each others' beliefs and values.
- **Resource sharing** – how much we help each other out, whether physically, emotionally, or financially.
- **Belief in family roles** – how much we see ourselves as members of a family and think families have an obligation to be loyal and kind to each other.
- **Structural convenience** – how easy it is to reach each other and whether we're well enough to visit.

The study found that all of these factors tended to reinforce each other – although they also found that how loving children are in adulthood tends to have more influence on parental feelings than the other way round. If you do have a difficult relationship with a child, don't overburden yourself with guilt: the science suggests that it's not all on you.

We don't have full control over every aspect of life, but we can control how much affection we show, how much we reach out to each other and, to some degree, how we communicate. The more solidarity you can build, the happier you all will be – both as individuals and as a family.

ACROSS THE GENERATIONS
THE ACTIVE GRANDPARENT

What's more delightful than a bouncing baby that you get to cuddle, coo over, and then hand back at the end of the day? Grandchildren, if you have them, can be one of life's greatest pleasures.

While it can be a little strange at first to hear someone calling you "Granddad" or "Nana" (surely you're not that old?), most of us adore our grandchildren – small (or not-so-small) people who can represent all the pleasures of parenting with none, or at least fewer, of the headaches. In earlier times, we might all have lived in the same villages or towns with a three-generation family within reach of each, but in an era where families tend to disperse, what's the best way to balance doting devotion with living your own life?

Enough time together?

Plenty of us do, in fact, see a lot of our grandchildren: in a period where childcare is expensive and most families can't support themselves on a single income, grandparent help can be the only thing that keeps a family going. Thirty per cent of US children whose mothers work outside the home are cared for on a regular basis by a grandma or grandpa, and in 2010 there was an official "grandparents' strike" in order to demonstrate just how much the economy rested on the older generation helping out by babysitting. Being a grandparent can be, quite literally, a serious business.

Secure relationships

If it's not possible for you to babysit, however, and you don't get to see your grandchildren regularly, does that mean you won't bond? In fact, psychological research suggests not. "Attachment", as it's technically called, isn't primarily correlated

> **I can love them** and send them home.
>
> Popular grandparenting motto

NOT A GRANDPARENT?

If grandchildren haven't happened for you, don't despair: a 2010 survey in England found that a supportive spouse or friendships made retirees happier, but whether or not they had grandchildren made little difference to their life satisfaction. If you have grandchildren, you love them, but if not, there are many other pleasures in life to enjoy.

to the amount of time you spend together: what gets a child attached is a caregiver who's reliably responsive to the needs they express. If you are empathic and trustworthy when the little one is around, that's enough to create a secure relationship – and of course, you can always call or video chat. (Today's generation are techno-babies, so they will probably grasp the idea of communicationg online much quicker than you do.)

Good memories

As the psychologist Nancy Kalish points out, children love repetition, so a few touchstones – a favourite in-joke, your famous hot chocolate – can be memories that sustain you both, even when your grandchildren have become adults themselves.

£4 billion

CHILDCARE COSTS

The UK charity Grandparents Plus estimates that the **childcare provided for free** by loving grans and granddads is worth £4 billion to the economy every year.

TO MOVE OR NOT TO MOVE?

Wanting to be nearer grandchildren is a major reason why retirees pack their bags and move house (see pp144–45). If your grandchildren are too far to visit, what are the pros and cons (see below) of moving?

How you work out a relationship with your grandchildren is a very personal choice, but there are as many good ways as there are families. Weigh up your options, pick what works for you, and enjoy your boys and girls.

Pros of moving	Cons of moving
You get to see the daily moments of their growing up.	You're leaving your familiar neighbourhood and network.
You're around for kisses, cuddles, and intimate bonding.	You might not like or be able to afford your children's area.
You have a support network on hand for daily help: there's nothing like a long babysitting history to make your son or daughter feel like they "owe" you some favours.	Babysitting is exhausting, and it's harder to "cry off" if you're only round the corner.
If you want advice from your children, they're in a better position to give it – not only are they on hand, but they're also much more aware of your practical circumstances.	If you and your children have personality clashes, those clashes will still be there when you live nearby. They may even be magnified because you can't get space from each other.
If your health fails, having spent time with your grandchildren beforehand makes it easier for them to see you as a loved relation rather than just a sick person they have to visit.	If you have more than one son or daughter with children, moving near one may cause resentment in the others.
If you find yourself widowed, you will have a lot more loved ones nearby.	Your children may not be permanently settled: if they have to move towns to follow the work, you could be stuck.

SAYING GOODBYE
DEALING WITH BEREAVEMENT

It would be wonderful if we didn't have to deal with death, but the reality is that as we age, we probably will lose loved ones — and this may include a spouse or partner. How can we deal with that heartbreak?

Most of us would prefer not to think about it, but the time comes when either we, our partners, or our loved ones have to face it: one of us will, eventually, have to go on without the other. Where do we turn when that happens?

The comfort of others

Studies support the common-sense theory that the warmer and more supportive the relationship, the more persistent our grief once the other person has gone. The most likely psychological explanation for this is "attachment" — a theory developed in the mid-twentieth century by pioneering researcher John Bowlby. Bowlby posited that human beings are interdependent rather than independent: we bond with a "special" person, are comforted by their presence, and feel distressed when we're separated.

We need empathy, caring, and responsiveness from people: when a partner is lost, being around other loved ones feeds the same part of our brain that's aching with the pain of separation — which lessens the ache. While the company of other loved ones won't fix everything, it does provide a cushion while we adjust.

Does religious faith help?

Bereavement leaves some of us wishing we believed in an afterlife; for others, our faith is supposed to be a comfort — but is it, empirically speaking? A 2007 study for *Palliative Medicine* magazine performed a synthesis of 32 studies, covering over 5,000 people. The results suggest that the answer is complicated: most, but not all, studies showed that religious faith made dealing with bereavement easier. Common comforts from religion include:

- Believing the loved one is at peace.
- Finding strength in prayer and rituals.
- Believing in an afterlife.
- Feeling support from a religious community.

If you find yourself unable to be consoled by your beliefs, seek comfort from other sources: family, friends, support groups, or a therapist or grief counsellor can all provide vital support.

Carrying on

Maintaining a lasting connection with lost loved ones is a different challenge for each of us. Your connection might be religious or mystical; one study found that approximately half of bereaved people "felt the presence" of a lost person; psychologists speculate that many of the other half may feel it too, but don't want to admit it for fear of looking foolish. For others, it might be a question of memories, legacy, or living on in their name. Bereavement is not an easy path, but most people find there's light at the end of it.

MOVING THROUGH GRIEF

The Kubler-Ross stages of grieving are well known: shock and denial followed by anger and guilt, bargaining, depression, and acceptance. However, more recent studies – such as the work of psychologist George Bonanno – propose that different people have different grief trajectories, as shown in the pie chart below. If you find yourself in the more chronic set, there's no shame in asking for help: living in constant pain helps no one.

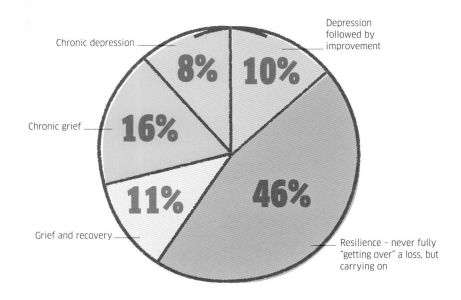

Chronic depression — 8%
Depression followed by improvement — 10%
Chronic grief — 16%
Grief and recovery — 11%
Resilience – never fully "getting over" a loss, but carrying on — 46%

LETTING GO?

If we believe in our need for attachment, letting the loved one "go" may not be the only answer. In 2007, psychologist J. William Worden proposed a four-stage process, also known as the "tear model":

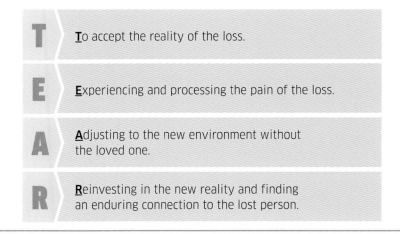

T **T**o accept the reality of the loss.

E **E**xperiencing and processing the pain of the loss.

A **A**djusting to the new environment without the loved one.

R **R**einvesting in the new reality and finding an enduring connection to the lost person.

THERE FOR SOMEONE
CARING FOR OTHERS

When you reach a certain age, there's a fair chance that someone you love – a spouse, a parent, or maybe a sibling – will have grown frail. If the caring devolves on you, what then?

When you hear the word "carer" or "caregiver", you may picture a professional – but in fact, unpaid carers in society do far more to look after sick and disabled people than any professional service. Sometimes, you have to be one yourself.

Not what you planned?
Disability isn't fair, and there is little doubt that you would prefer to spend your hard-earned retirement with a healthy loved one. Caring is a tiring job, so keep an eye on your own mental health – especially if you had to retire early to take it on: data from the US Health and Retirement Study published in the *Journal of Gerontology* suggests that it is women in this position who are particularly vulnerable to depression.

That said, whatever your circumstances – male or female, early or late retiree, and no matter how much you love the person you're looking after, you may find it tiring and frustrating at times. It's important to make sure you don't neglect your own needs.

Taking care of yourself
Caregivers aren't superhuman, and nobody can manage without paying some attention to their own wellbeing.

Firstly, take care of yourself physically. There's a good chance you'll be doing some heavy hauling, and that's hard enough

6.5 million

THE INVISIBLE ARMY

In 2015, Carers UK estimated there were 6.5 million **carers in the UK**. Caring, though often unobserved, is a huge part of society.

on a spry twenty-year-old spine, never mind yours. Professional carers often have training to show them the best ways to lift: talk to a doctor or physiotherapist and make sure your technique is safe for you as well as the person you're caring for. Book regular check-ups to make sure you're not straining your body, and research and apply for any equipment that might make your life easier.

Secondly, ask for help. If your loved one lives for a long time, realistically you will get weaker over the years. Bring in family members as much as you can, and carer charities are your best resource when it comes to making plans for the future. You may also be eligible for financial support, so claim whatever you can.

Above all: value yourself. A 2011 study took a detailed look at carers' coping methods

and concluded that, far from being helpless victims of circumstance, carers were "proactive and determined": problem-solving, establishing priorities, and spending time thinking about things other than caring were strategies they used well. Caring is a job, and it's hard work, but give yourself some respect: the research confirms that most caregivers aren't just loyal, but smart and capable as well.

THE CARE PLAN

In an emergency, or if you need a break (carer respite is something a lot of charities try to provide), will your loved one be OK? Set up an emergency plan so someone can fill in for you in your absence – carer charities can help with this – and keep it somewhere in the house that's easy to find. Plans should include various items, such as those listed below, and any special needs.

The person's daily routine.
A list of medications.
Ongoing treatments such as physiotherapy.
Diet – what they can eat, and also what they prefer.
Contact details for family and friends.
Contact details for your doctor and any other medical professionals.

If you know you can tell helpers "The care plan is in the top drawer of the desk", that can make things much simpler in a crisis.

A CARER'S CARD

What if something happens to you while your loved one is home alone? Some carer charities issue a card that you can carry with you at all times. It states that you're a carer, that someone depends on you, and gives contact details for your emergency back-up. If you can't find a charity that provides a card, get one printed yourself: it will be a weight off your mind to know that the person you care for will be looked after no matter what.

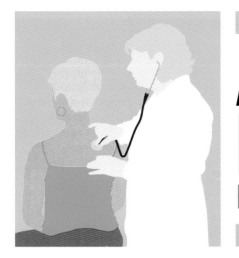

ACCEPTING LIMITATIONS
DEALING WITH HEALTH CONCERNS

Living to a ripe old age almost always means living with some health issues. The key is not to hope for perfect wellness, but to develop our ability to enjoy life despite any limitations.

Nobody wants to feel old and sick. Ironically, the better modern medicine becomes, the more likely that is: we live longer, which means we live long enough to develop chronic conditions. How do we stop illness from spoiling our pleasure in life entirely?

Dealing with stress
There is no question that health problems are stressful. A key theory in how seniors cope with medical issues is US psychologist Leonard Pearlin's "psychosocial process model". The idea behind this is that our own resources and the ways in which we cope are the major player in how we determine our emotional outcome.

What can we do to get the best outcome? Psychologists Margret and Paul Baltes developed an influential concept known as the Selection, Optimization, and Compensation model (see opposite), which shows the processes retirees go through.

Can we learn resilience?
A concept that psychologists discuss a lot when it comes to coping with health problems is "resilience" – by which they mean the ability to suffer misfortune and discomfort without becoming too badly discouraged. It's easy to think of resilience as a personality trait that we either have or we don't – but can it be cultivated? Recent research suggests that it can – that resilience, rather than

being a fixed trait, may be a skill you can learn. A 2008 study published in *Sociology of Health and Illness*, for example, identified several key methods resilient people tended to use:

- They told stories of their lives that compared their current adversities to misfortunes they'd had – and coped with – before, meaning that they could consider themselves copers rather than victims.
- As far as possible, they maintained old social roles and activities that gave them pleasure and confidence.
- They relied on tried and tested coping strategies, which further supported their identity as people who could deal with what life threw at them.
- They drew support from the people close to them.

Ill health can limit what we do, but we generally feel better if we accept it as just one more

SHAPING YOUR GOALS

As late psychologists Margret and Paul Baltes discovered, if someone is faced with a medical condition that has an impact on their daily life, they usually experience a three-step process in accepting and adjusting their routines and choice of pursuits, as follows:

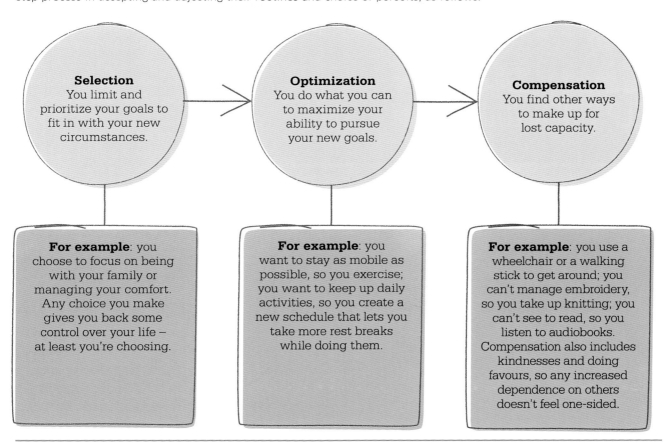

Selection
You limit and prioritize your goals to fit in with your new circumstances.

Optimization
You do what you can to maximize your ability to pursue your new goals.

Compensation
You find other ways to make up for lost capacity.

For example: you choose to focus on being with your family or managing your comfort. Any choice you make gives you back some control over your life – at least you're choosing.

For example: you want to stay as mobile as possible, so you exercise; you want to keep up daily activities, so you create a new schedule that lets you take more rest breaks while doing them.

For example: you use a wheelchair or a walking stick to get around; you can't manage embroidery, so you take up knitting; you can't see to read, so you listen to audiobooks. Compensation also includes kindnesses and doing favours, so any increased dependence on others doesn't feel one-sided.

incident that forms the history of "war stories" in our lives and if we keep doing what we love and being with the people we love as much as we can. In other words, we feel most resilient when we resist letting medical problems strip away our identity or allow them to significantly change our outlook. Nobody looks forward to poor health – but we can develop the ability to feel like ourselves right up until our last days.

Q FINDING THE RIGHT DOCTOR

A good medical professional makes all the difference to your quality of life; one 2007 survey found that patients who had good communication with their doctors had lower blood pressure. Look out for these key points:

- Your doctor really listens and takes you seriously when you report symptoms.
- You have faith in their competence.

- You feel treated like a person, not a set of symptoms.
- They appreciate that your wellbeing is part of the treatment.
- You can contact them when you need to without being made to feel like a nuisance.
- They respect your right to a second opinion and refer you quickly.

IN THEIR HANDS

HELP WHEN YOU NEED IT

However much we wish it otherwise, the human body doesn't last forever. For most, there will be a period where we can no longer manage alone, and have to resign ourselves to the care of others.

We'd probably all prefer to live to a hundred in perfect health and then die quietly in our sleep one night, but if we're not that fortunate, we'll need to adjust to a period where our health gets worse and we need help from other people to keep us going. How do we manage that difficult time?

Afraid to be a burden?

For most of us, our independence is highly prized – not just because it's a source of pride, but also because we don't want to trouble our loved ones. A quarter of the participants in a 2010 Canadian study on stroke survivors, for example, reported that they kept quiet about their feelings or resisted asking for help for fear of distressing the relations who were caring for them. The same study found that, while looking after the subjects undoubtedly was an effort, the stroke survivors

65%

FEELINGS OF GUILT

According to a review of studies by *Palliative Medicine* magazine, up to 65 per cent of terminally ill people report **worrying that they're a "burden"** on their family.

tended to overestimate just how burdensome their loved ones found them: troubling our families seems to weigh excessively on our consciences.

How much this worries you may be partly cultural: if you come from a background with what a 2009 US study called a "traditional caregiving ideology" – where there's more expectation that the young care for the old – accepting care can feel more like you're occupying an expected role than violating one – but even so, everyone in that study found it frustrating to be dependent, regardless of culture. What we're talking about is known as "equity theory": we prefer it if our relationships are reciprocal, and we feel uncomfortable when we need to accept more than we can give. Those people who decide to move from home care to a more professional environment, such as assisted living and retirement homes, are often partly motivated by the desire to "spare" their families from caregiving duties they don't feel able to repay.

Help from a partner

Most of us (see above, right) would prefer to be cared for in our own homes, which usually means getting help from a partner. But we need the right kind of help. As a 1998 study in the *International Journal of Behavioral Development* explains, a "caregiving" spouse might be uninvolved or controlling,

WHERE TO GO?

If you need to be cared for, where would you choose to be? In a 2013 survey, "baby boomers" (those born between 1946 and 1964) with a mid-range income were asked what they'd prefer – here's what they said:

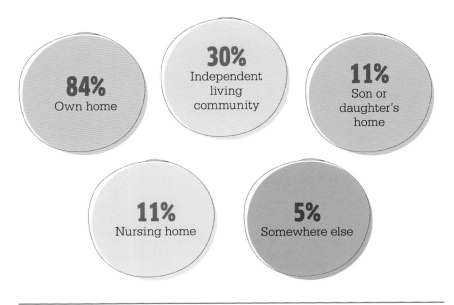

84% Own home

30% Independent living community

11% Son or daughter's home

11% Nursing home

5% Somewhere else

supportive or collaborative – and it's collaboration that we really thrive on. Psychologists call it "dyadic coping". Put simply: the best help a partner can give is to view "your problem" as "our problem", and address it with you as a loving equal.

Support without collaboration can be a mixed blessing: as a 2002 US study of women supported by their spouses tactfully put it, "their assistance is not always perceived as helpful by recipients". The women whose partners viewed them as helpless tended to be less confident and more prone to depression and self-neglect: we need to feel some sense of control

over how we're supported. How independent you were to begin with is also a key factor: too much "support" for a very independent-minded person can actually make you feel worse.

In the end, being cared for balances what's most important to us: our need for physical comfort and safety, and our need to be viewed as an equal by those around us. You will need to communicate what's essential to give you a sense of dignity, but the more a supportive caregiver respects your need for equality – not just helping you, but knowing when not to help – the more at peace everyone will be.

CHAPTER 6

THE NEW YOU

HOW TO REINVENT YOURSELF

WHERE NEXT?

ASSESSING YOUR POTENTIAL

What do you really want to do? Who have you always really wanted to be? Retirement isn't just about practical planning: it can be a chance to spend time on what matters to you most.

O nce you settle into retirement, does everything have to be a matter of pottering around and filling in the time? Far from it. Today's retirees are healthier, more active, and more lively minded than ever before: retirement can be nothing less than a period where you have all the time you want to develop your own identity.

The rainbow model

Can you picture your life as a rainbow? No, this isn't New Age spirituality, this is science: in 1990, the psychologist Donald Super proposed the model of the "life-career rainbow" as a way to envisage our lives. The way it worked was this: different aspects of our lives formed different "colours" – working, learning, being a friend, being a parent, all shade into each other but retain distinct

Q IS PEACE AND QUIET ALL BAD?

Do you have to stay busy to stay happy? Actually, it seems not: a study by Australian psychologists Y.D. Wells and H.L. Kendig found that people who'd retired within the past five years were more likely to report decreased physical and social activity – but increased happiness. Sometimes "taking it easy" might just mean cutting out the hard work and focusing on what we like best.

qualities of their own – and the arc of the rainbow follows four distinct stages:

- **Growth** – we start on a new aspect of life.
- **Exploration** – we develop our connections and understanding.
- **Establishment** – it becomes a full part of our existence.
- **Disengagement** – we start to step back.

In Super's original theory, retirement was pictured as a stage of disengagement. More recently, however, psychologists are starting to challenge this view – notably, Charles P. Chen of the University of Toronto.

In 2011, Chen published a paper arguing that "disengagement" was an outmoded image of retirement: instead, he suggested, a better concept was "re-engagement". Rather than giving up on our old life and stopping there, we use retirement as a period of creativity, when we stop worrying about the nine-to-five and start thinking about our real vocation, what gives us a sense of genuine fulfilment and meaning. This, Chen wrote, could be a "lengthy and colourful life experience": retirement can be "dynamic and multifaceted" if we choose to pursue things that really interest us.

A new you – or the true you?

Many of us (though not all) actually did love our jobs, and were happy with the sense of

WHAT REALLY INTERESTS YOU?

A 2004 survey of retirees' aspirations by Prudential Investment estimates that among the over-55s in the UK:

1.6 million
...plan to spend a lot of time golfing.

2.1 million
...plan to take up painting.

7.8 million
...want to become "gap year grannies and granddads" by travelling the world.

1.3 million
...would like to write a novel.

8 million
...want to see more of their friends and go to more restaurants, pubs, and dinner parties.

Seeing people and pursuing self-development were high on the agenda. Is there something you've always longed to try?

identity that our career gave us. If that was you, however, it doesn't necessarily mean you'll be unhappy in retirement. Rather than seeing your happiness with work as entirely created by the job, think of the capacity to enjoy work as a transferrable skill that you can now apply to new things.

If, on the other hand, your job really wasn't much fun, retirement is the time when you can cast off the shackles and start trying activities you actually want to do. Exactly what those will be is up to you – but once you're retired, you will have the time to explore them.

COLLECTIVE ACTION
JOINING UP WITH FELLOW RETIREES

We all know that friendship can be critical to a happy life. However, we shouldn't underestimate the importance of *fellowship* – the comfort of shared activity with like-minded people.

People often advise retirees to get involved in volunteer activity – which can be anything from operating the till at a charity shop to lobbying for a political cause. Usually we're told that it's good because it keeps us "mentally active", which is undoubtedly true, but there's another benefit as well: it gets us involved with other people who share at least some of our interests.

Social activities
Do you have to have a cause to have fellowship? Not at all – or rather, when you're retired and looking to create a new sense of meaning, creating it with other retirees is a cause in itself. You might prefer to join a club of some kind or to have an arrangement with old friends – there's nothing like getting together to share memories to create a sense of solidarity – but whether you do it formally or informally, retirees who organize events that bring them together just for fun are doing everyone a favour. After all, being able to enjoy oneself after a lifetime of hard work is definitely a deserving mission.

Sharing a principle
Short of local friends? Well, there's a great value in helping out with local causes. In 1954, a Turkish-US social psychologist named Muzafer Sherif performed his famous "Robbers Cave" experiment. Working with a group of boys at a summer camp in Robbers Cave State Park in Oklahoma, USA, he divided them into two groups and let them choose their own names.

The "Rattlers" and the "Eagles", set into competition by Sherif, grew increasingly hostile with each other – yet when presented with some shared "problems" that they couldn't solve except by working together (such as fixing the water supply and clubbing together to afford a movie) their antagonism melted away. The boys joined forces, and by the end of the trip, they all cheered at the

> Never doubt that **a small group** of thoughtful, committed citizens can change the world.
>
> **Margaret Mead**
> Cultural anthropologist

prospect of sharing the bus home, and decided to spend the money won in earlier competitions against each other on milkshakes for everyone. Working together on a shared problem had created friendships in short order.

Shared achievement

Obviously retirees aren't boys at summer camp, but Sherif's research remains crucial to social psychology in general. The "superordinate goal" (something that can only be achieved by working together – see pp120–21) can create a sense of satisfaction at work – but Sherif's findings show that it's not really the goal itself that matters. The "broken" water supply and inability to "afford" a movie were quite artificial. There's no point working on something you don't believe in, but psychology suggests that if you're short of "like-minded" people in your local area, finding even one point where you have to work together may forge new bonds where none existed before.

We don't lose our desire to be with people when we retire – and one of the greatest satisfactions in being around other people is a sense of shared achievement. That achievement could be as solid as campaigning for better traffic control in your area or as simple as being part of a fun place for retirees to go, but whatever appeals to you, don't forget the power of friends and allies.

HOW MANY ACTIVITIES SHOULD WE DO?

Should we do a hundred activities, or just one or two? A 2005 study for the American National Institute on Aging surveyed a group of more than 1,000 over-60s to find out how happy they were and how satisfied they were with life relative to how much "productive activity" – which included volunteering – they did. The results showed that the happiest were those who had a fair amount going on, but not too much. On the other hand, too few activities could result in someone showing symptoms of depression. The study concluded that over-60s who pursued beetween four and five productive activities were happiest, most satisfied with life, and showed only 0–1 symptoms of depression.

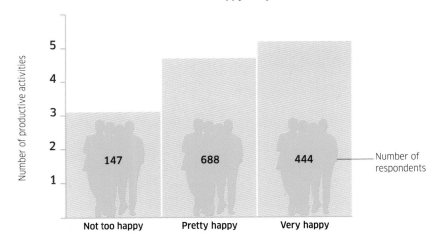

How happy are you?

Number of respondents

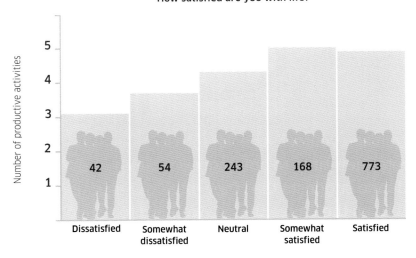

How satisfied are you with life?

IN PLACE OF WORK

MAKING A CONTRIBUTION

Do you see yourself as a volunteer? Many retirees devote their time to doing good works – and the evidence suggests that they often get as much benefit as the cause they're working to support.

If you still have plenty of energy and want a sense of purpose in your life, there might be a soup kitchen, animal shelter, veterans' organization, political campaign, or tour guide position with your name on it.

Doing well by doing good

In 2004, US psychologist Linda Fried and her team described volunteering as the "social model of health promotion". Volunteer work, according to Fried, is good for older people because it keeps them physically, socially, and cognitively active. Of course, many self-improvement projects such as exercise regimes try to do this, but they tend to have a high drop-off rate by the six-month mark. Volunteer work, as Fried found has an impressive "retention rate" of 80 per cent.

Part of this may be because people tend to choose causes that are rewarding as well as

Q DUTY BOUND?

It's important not to volunteer for anything you don't enjoy. A 2012 study published in *The Gerontologist* found that people who felt "low to medium engagement" with their volunteer work were psychologically worse off than people who didn't volunteer at all. If you enjoy it, the benefits can be great, but don't sacrifice your quality of life just because you feel you "should".

worthwhile; in fact, the psychologist Robert Stebbins described volunteering as a form of "serious leisure" in the same class as hobbies, sports, and the arts, meaning that it can be a win-win for you and for your chosen cause.

Meeting people

Retirees are often urged to make new friends; volunteering can be a good way to do it. Not only does it give you a sense of fellowship (see pp188–89); it also stands a good chance of giving you the opportunity to meet nice people. Studies confirm that retired volunteers tend to be among the healthiest and most sociable of all retirees, and further research suggests that retirees are likely to have a different investment in volunteer work. Retirees usually tend to volunteer to stay active and help people – and so are particularly likely to volunteer for social or community projects where they can meet the people they're helping directly.

Most retirees don't do volunteer work, but when they do, they tend to get very involved (see right). What cause or role appeals to you most will of course depend on your own values.

Before you sign up

One activity that's often marketed at volunteers is "voluntourism" – where you travel abroad to do charity work. However, some

WHAT'S IN IT FOR YOU?

Studies have documented a whole host of benefits that can be gained from volunteering in retirement, including:

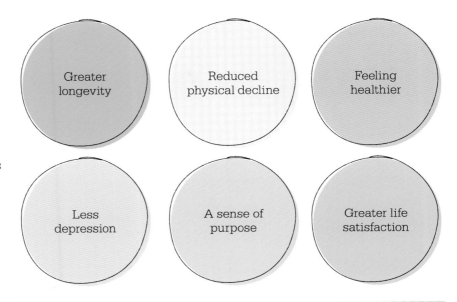

Greater longevity

Reduced physical decline

Feeling healthier

Less depression

A sense of purpose

Greater life satisfaction

ethical groups have argued that the practice can do more harm than good. Voluntourists who join a building project, for example, are often unskilled and likely to be taking employment away from local people. Time spent in orphanages can actually hurt the children emotionally: children need stable long-term relationships, and bonding with people who then go home can leave them more insecure than ever. Add to this the fact that a lot of unscrupulous people set up fake charities, and the voluntourism business is a complicated one at best. This isn't to say that all voluntourist projects are bad, but if the idea interests you, research it very carefully before you commit.

23.6%

GIVE A HELPING HAND

The 2014 US Bureau of Labor Statistics estimated that 23.6 per cent of over-65s **did some formal volunteering**, which is less than most other age groups, but at a mean of 96 hours per year, retirees clocked up over double the national average in terms of time spent.

96 hours

PLEASANT HOURS

HOBBIES OLD AND NEW

Retirement is a great time to invest in old interests, or to challenge yourself and try something unfamiliar; now that you're free from work obligations, you can decide for yourself how to spend your days.

People talk a lot about hobbies when you retire – and with good reason, because spending more time doing the things you love is one of the biggest benefits of life beyond work. If you've always been longing to spend more time with your carving tools or your cross-stitch then you may already have a good idea about what you'd like to do with your time. If you're not sure, however, or relish the chance to try new things, the flexibility of retirement gives you the perfect opportunity to branch out.

Sports for fun

As a society, we tend to have conflicting messages about the aging body: there's pressure to stay "young-looking" and medical advice about staying fit, yet we often have (exaggerated) anxieties that gentle exercise is all we're supposed to be capable of past a certain age. Surveys in Canada, Australia, New Zealand, the UK, and the US all suggest that retirees tend to underestimate how much exercise they need to keep healthy and independent, and ageist ideas that we're "past it" are likely to contribute to this misapprehension. It's enough to discourage anyone, let alone if sports have never been your thing.

Keeping physically active has tremendous positive effects, not just on your body but on your

EXERCISE FOR THE MIND

Exercise is good for your mind as well as your body. The Association for Applied Sport Psychology in the US suggests the following common psychological benefits of exercise:

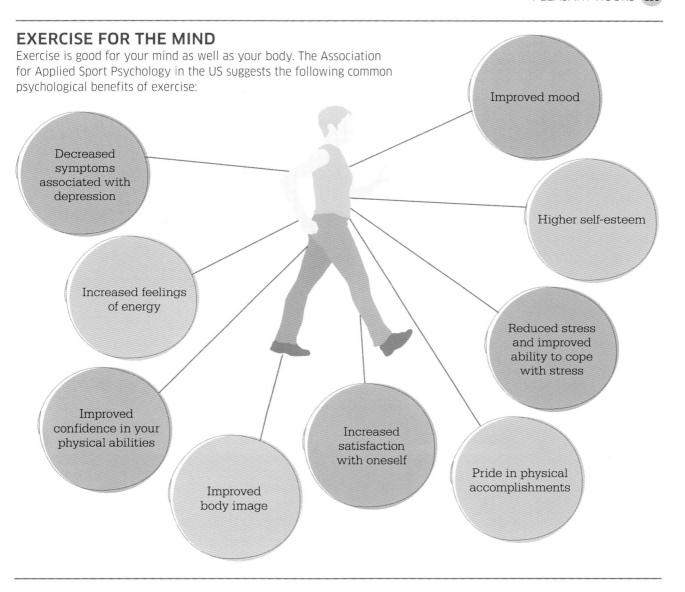

Improved mood

Decreased symptoms associated with depression

Higher self-esteem

Increased feelings of energy

Reduced stress and improved ability to cope with stress

Improved confidence in your physical abilities

Increased satisfaction with oneself

Improved body image

Pride in physical accomplishments

spirits too – psychologists call it the "feel better phenomenon". While it's OK to be competitive if you feel like it, retirement gives you the freedom to simply enjoy physical activities rather than trying to "be the best" at them; nobody will expect you to make the Olympic team! Don't let the stereotypes hold you back: plenty of communities have local sport teams, which are a great way to make new friends as well as stay active. If you don't feel up to taking the field, however, there are other ways to exercise; walking, hiking, gardening, and cycling are all good options that will get your heart pumping and give you time to appreciate the great outdoors.

Feeling artistic?

Painting, writing, learning musical instruments – all are popular retirement activities, and with good reason: the arts give you the freedom to do something meaningful and rewarding, control over what you make or play, and the pride of creating something you're happy with.

Q DO YOU NEED A CHANGE?

If you're already involved in activities you love, do you have to try new things? Research suggests not. A 2007 Israeli study found that retirees fell into one of four groups when it came to their attitudes towards hobbies and activities:

Concentrators – who stuck to the same activities but did them more.

Expanders – who participated in more activities and at a higher rate.

Diffusers – who participated in more activities, but none of them very much.

Reducers – who did fewer activities or the same ones less frequently.

The happiest were the concentrators, followed by the expanders, the diffusers, and then the reducers. The reducers were the least happy, in part, because their "reducing" was due to health problems or limited opportunities. If you think you're in this camp, seek out organizations that can bring your hobbies to you, or try connecting with fellow enthusiasts over the Internet. Intensifying your focus or enlarging your activities seem to be retirees' keys to the good life.

A team of German neurologists conducted a study in 2014 to assess the impact of visual art on retired people's brains, and found that painting and drawing improved interaction between certain regions of the brain; studies have shown that similar neurological benefits can come from other forms of creative expression, too. If you're hesitating between different arts, which are your best options?

Try picking an art form that's intrinsically rewarding rather than one that depends on circumstances beyond your control. If you enjoy writing, for example, then it can be a delight, but if your aim is to create a bestselling novel, you may find yourself frustrated – publication and good sales are something no one can guarantee. Similarly, if you learn an instrument because of a love of music, you're on more secure ground than if your aim is to become a professional musician. Joining a community painting group or an orchestra can be great fun, of course, but make sure that your primary reward is the pleasure of making or doing the art itself: that way,

your enjoyment of it depends on nothing but yourself. It's possible you might have a further great career ahead of you, of course, but choose something that will feel like time well spent even if it's just you and your work: that way, you can't lose.

Mastery and happiness
One of the joys of life is what psychologists call "mastery": the feeling that you're capable of something, and that you know what you're doing (see pp58–59). Hobbies can be the perfect way to master something new, or to

GETTING CRAFTY

Few things are more satisfying than seeing something take shape in your own hands. Here are some ideas to consider:

- Building models (boats, trains, castles etc.)
- Pressing flowers
- Woodwork
- Sewing and embroidery
- Felting
- Knitting and crochet
- Jewellery making
- Pottery
- Quilting and patchwork
- Stained glass
- Mosaic making
- Paper cutting
- Making home-made beer or wine
- Soap making
- Candle making
- Baking and cake decorating

CREATURE COMFORTS

If you're a dog-lover and you're fit enough to face the daily walks, you'll already know how much fun it can be to meet other owners out on your rambles – but if the pleasure of owning a pet really inspires you, you might look into pet shows. It's not just dogs and cats that go to exhibits: birds, fish, and reptiles all have their own events – there's even rabbit show-jumping!

If you don't own your own animal, however, it doesn't stop there – you could try volunteering at a local shelter. Don't overlook the pleasures of wild creatures either: even a small garden has space for a bird-feeder and nesting box (and if you feel like some DIY, making them yourself can be fun). If that's not possible, a pair of binoculars might be all you need. Urban birdwatching is on the rise, for example, and there may be more to see in a built-up area than you'd expect; many nature reserves have wheelchair-accessible boardwalks, too.

raise old abilities to new heights, which is tremendously good for our self-esteem. The word "hobby" can sound a bit dismissive – it has an air of "just a hobby", just something we do to fill the time – but in fact a skilled and happy hobbyist is pursuing one of the greatest psychological secrets to success we know. Find things you enjoy, and there's a good chance that your confidence and wellbeing will increase along with your accomplishments, keeping you not just occupied, but contented with life and with yourself.

A ROUND OF GOLF?

The retiree strolling round the golf course is **practically a stereotype**, but there's good foundation for it. The National Golf Foundation of North America estimates that:

61%

...of golfers are over 50 and

37%

...are over 60.

WHERE GENERATIONS MEET

When it comes to crafts, a lot of the "traditional" hobbies are enjoying a fashion revival; knitting and crochet, in particular, are popular among young people.

If you're fond of a traditional craft but don't want to leave the modern world behind, try going online (see pp148-51): chances are you'll be able to share skills with a whole range of ages. Passing on your experience to younger generations, and in turn being inspired by their enthusiasm and creativity, can be a great boost to your motivation and self-worth.

HAPPINESS FOR REAL
REDEFINING THE GOOD LIFE

You might expect happiness to be found in the freeing up of time in retirement – like a pot of gold at the end of a rainbow. In reality, you will need to be prepared to define or re-evaluate your goals.

Many expect happiness to be an automatic consequence when the tedium or responsibility they associate with work is lifted from their shoulders. The fallacy here is the equation of happiness with leisure – whereas, in fact, leisure in itself is neutral: a medium, not an emotional state.

Happiness is usually many-sided. Surveys by psychologists suggest it tends to be based on good relationships, an active life and a sense of purpose, as well as escaping extreme poverty or ill-health. The activity may be mental, not physical, and people who find it difficult to get around often report being happy if they have found rewarding things to do with their time.

Activity, purpose, and love

A "sense of purpose" often comes from activities such as gardening, painting, music, volunteering, study, and forms of exercise, but it could be anything from writing to maintaining a vintage steam engine. Grandparenting often gives pleasure. Caregiving is supremely purposeful, and carers may find happiness in a loving relationship with the dependent.

There are dreams we don't expect to realize and dreams we do. Try to recognize the former, rather than adding them to the second category just because you now have more time. However, the pursuit of a realistic ambition can make us happy, especially when there is satisfaction to be gained on the way.

Psychologists recognize that loving relationships are an important basis of wellbeing, and the maturing of a relationship into old age is precious and inspiring, although new love can also be fulfilling. Many profound thinkers on the subject of love would extend the definition to cover a compassionate and forgiving relationship with our fellow human beings. There is also great value to be found in the broader and more elusive notion of the "good life", however an individual might define that term (see opposite).

Three types of happiness

The US philosopher Robert Nozick distinguished between circumstantial happiness (such as getting married or winning a competition), process happiness (from experiences of people, places and things) and "life satisfaction" (being generally pleased with life). Applying

WHAT DOES THE GOOD LIFE LOOK LIKE?

Exactly what constitutes the good life has been much debated by philosophers. Despite a great deal of disagreement, certain broad themes have won support from many important thinkers. Our faithfulness, in practice, to an ideal of the good life is likely to be a pillar of our happiness.

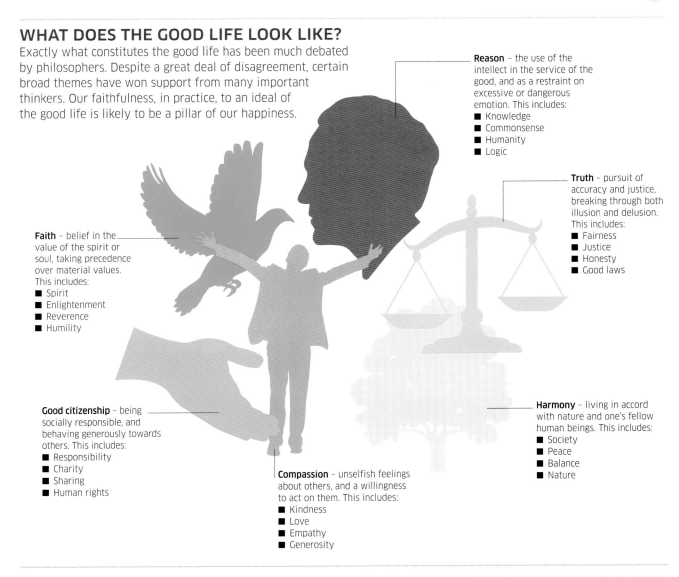

Reason – the use of the intellect in the service of the good, and as a restraint on excessive or dangerous emotion. This includes:
- Knowledge
- Commonsense
- Humanity
- Logic

Truth – pursuit of accuracy and justice, breaking through both illusion and delusion. This includes:
- Fairness
- Justice
- Honesty
- Good laws

Faith – belief in the value of the spirit or soul, taking precedence over material values. This includes:
- Spirit
- Enlightenment
- Reverence
- Humility

Good citizenship – being socially responsible, and behaving generously towards others. This includes:
- Responsibility
- Charity
- Sharing
- Human rights

Compassion – unselfish feelings about others, and a willingness to act on them. This includes:
- Kindness
- Love
- Empathy
- Generosity

Harmony – living in accord with nature and one's fellow human beings. This includes:
- Society
- Peace
- Balance
- Nature

these yardsticks to retirement, it is possible to discern three rules: do not expect to find happiness in quitting work, only in what you can make happen afterwards; seek rich experiences; and value as much of love, health and achievement as are available. By doing this within the limits of what is within your reach, you are likely to achieve happiness.

🔍 FINDING A ROUTE TO HAPPINESS

In retirement we can spend more time on pursuits that take us towards "self-actualization" – happiness as a destination of personal development. Psychologist Carl Jung coined the term "individuation" – realizing our potential with the help of enhanced self-awareness.

In order to become the best you can be, answer these questions:

- Which areas of life give me my identity, my roles?
- In those areas of life, what goals would I like to achieve?
- Among these different options, what are my priorities?

BACK TO SCHOOL
LEARNING AFTER 60

Learning doesn't stop at school – it continues throughout our lives. After retirement, learning helps give meaning and purpose to your life, leads you into worthwhile experiences, and boosts your self-esteem.

Studying a subject, learning a new skill, or developing an existing one, are wonderful ways to meet some of the practical and psychological needs of retirement. Most simply, you finally have time for learning, which is endlessly involving. More than that, psychologists have shown that the stimulation provided by a course of study or training is the perfect antidote to the purposelessness many retired people fear. If you miss the distinction between weekends and weekdays, learning can restore that distinction if you study most days but choose to take weekends "off". However, even setting aside, say, ten hours a week to learning is enough to make a difference. You can provide your retirement with a clear sense of structure, and this helps especially in the early years, when the relaxation of time constraints may leave you struggling to come to terms with your new lifestyle.

Q WHAT MOTIVATES OLDER LEARNERS?

According to a 2004 US study, the top two reasons for going back to school in retirement are:

■ **Cognitive interest** – that is, the sheer pleasure of learning.

■ **Social contact** – meeting new people and making new friends.

The best adult education, one would hope, allows you to achieve both.

Learning styles for all

Formal study or training and working towards an exam or certificate will suit you if you crave a marked sense of achievement. People often miss this on leaving work. Along with achievement, of course, comes purpose: striving is meaningful in itself. Informal study may suit you better, especially if you have irregular demands placed on your time. This is also partly a matter of temperament: do you lean towards systematic learning or a freestyle approach?

Solo learning has the advantage of complete flexibility, but learning with others, in a class or workshop, may suit you if you crave company. Making friends on a course has psychological benefits, building up a social network as well as feeding back into your learning, through shared perspectives. Self-understanding will reduce the possibilities of signing up to an unsuitable commitment.

The learning environment

A 2008 US study pinpointed three qualities that particularly suit retirees in a classroom:

- **Interactive teaching**. Being able to talk about your own experiences and views in class can be more rewarding than sitting passively listening. Look for classes that have structured discussion time.
- **Good instructors**. Retired students prefer teachers who

are enthusiastic, clear, well-informed, and respectful of their students' opinions and abilities. Instructors who make the learning experience comfortable and low-pressure are also popular. Probably everyone would prefer that, of course,

TWO TYPES OF SMART

Is there only one way to be clever? According to English psychologist Raymond Cattell, there are two types of intelligence that form part of our intellectual development – and of those two, one lasts longer:

- **Fluid intelligence** – this is about problem-solving, thinking in the abstract, and coming up with alternative perspectives.
- **Crystallized Intelligence** – this is about acquired knowledge, both from previous learning and from past experiences.

Neither kind is "better"; they're complementary, and we use both. However, as the graph below shows, fluid intelligence peaks sooner, whereas crystallized intelligence keeps growing throughout life – so even if you do find yourself less patient with abstract problems or struggling to remember someone's name, your brain will keep adding to its stock as long as you keep feeding it interesting information.

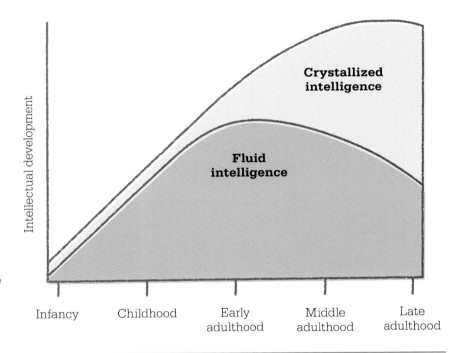

but in retirement you shouldn't put up with anything less.
- **Relevant topics**. Retirees usually choose subjects that have some connection to their own lives; a totally new subject can often be less appealing than one with an obvious application.

PASSING ON THE FLAME
TEACHING A NEW GENERATION

Do you feel you've got some knowledge worth sharing? Psychology suggests that the more we support the younger generation through their adulthood, the better use we feel we've made of our own.

In 1959, German psychologist Erik Erikson proposed the theory of "psychosocial development". Rather than simply reaching adulthood and stopping, Erikson believed we faced a series of "crises" as we mature, those situations where our developing understanding comes up against the world – and we have to make decisions about how we see the world and our place within it.

You can see a detailed view of his stages of life opposite – but for the purposes of retirement, psychologists agree that the most important concept in Erikson's work is the idea of "generativity" – that is, of turning our experience, wisdom and resources into generosity and guidance for the next generation.

Generativity as a concept

Numerous studies have found that, far from being self-sacrificing, living a "generative" retirement is actually the key to happiness: people who provide support for younger protégées are more likely to feel they're aging successfully.

Generativity is a broad concept. In 1984, for instance, psychologist John Kotre expanded on Erikson's theories to propose four variants:

- **Biological** – having and raising children.
- **Parental** – nurturing, disciplining and loving children (whether your biological offspring or not).
- **Technical** – passing on your skills and expertise.
- **Cultural** – passing on your wisdom and experience.

In 2002, US psychologist George Eman Vaillant proposed that one of the best roles for an older adult was the "keeper of meaning", and that this in itself is a form of generativity. What "meaning" means to you will be a matter of personal values, but the science suggests that you'll be happiest if you use it to support the young.

Generativity in practice

How do we live out this virtue? Probably all of us have been in situations where the next generation don't actually want our guidance, so it tests our

> To keep it, you have to **give it away**.
>
> **George Eman Vaillant**
> US psychologist

THE STAGES OF LIFE

Erik Erikson divided life into eight different stages, each with its own questions and strengths. In retirement, generativity can be the foundation of real happiness.

Life stage	Age	Key question	Basic virtue	Quality we seek
Infancy	Birth to 18 months	Can I trust the people around me?	Hope	Trust
Early childhood	1½ to 3	Can I do things for myself or am I dependent on others?	Will	Autonomy
Play age	3 to 6	Am I good or bad?	Purpose	Initiative
School age	5 to 12	How can I be good?	Competence	Industry
Adolescence	12 to 18	Who am I?	Fidelity	Identity
Young adulthood	18 to 40	Will I be loved or alone?	Love	Intimacy
Adulthood	40 to 65	How can I contribute to the world?	Care	Generativity
Maturity	65 onwards	Have I lived a meaningful life?	Wisdom	Integrity

ingenuity to find the best ways. Being a good citizen has been found to be surprisingly effective, such as participating in politics, or neighbourhood activities; even paying taxes without complaint creates a sense of generativity. However, a 2008 US study discovered that retirees tended to seek out activities that gave them a sense of agency and competence as well as creating benefits for the next generation. After all, if you're passing on your sense of meaning, you'll want to do it in an area you find meaningful.

Some of us find enough generativity in caring for and supporting our families, while others prefer public action. Whatever you choose, the evidence suggests that supporting and guiding the next generation is very satisfying.

IN THE GREEN ROOM
GARDENING AND NATURE

There are few more iconic images of retirement than the contented gardener digging in the sun. If you're feeling green fingered, maybe it's time to head outside and pick up your spade.

Gardening, as they say, is good for the soul, and this seems to be empirically true: one 2010 study published in *Environmental Health* found that even after adjusting for income, education, gender, and life stress, older gardeners were more active, as well as healthier and happier than their non-gardening contemporaries – a much greater difference than among younger people. Even if you've never been much of a gardener before, now might be the time to start thinking green.

Gardening for health

Working in the garden isn't just pottering; it's a good way to get gentle, non-joint-straining cardiovascular exercise. Studies have suggested that retirees who exercise a few times a week are

Q PLAYING SAFE

You want your garden to be a healing space, so take a few basic precautions:

- Wear gloves for rough work.
- Apply sunscreen and wear long sleeves and a hat in hot weather.
- Make sure your digging technique doesn't overstrain your back.
- Make sure you lift heavy items correctly.
- Stay up to date with your tetanus jabs in case you cut yourself.
- Keep your tools clean and rust-free.
- Treat any scratches before they get infected.

up to 2.5 times less likely to suffer serious health problems, and 45 minutes of gardening can burn as many calories as half an hour of aerobics. Meanwhile, the American Horticultural Therapy Association reports that if you're recovering from an illness, digging and planting improves your balance, coordination, and strength, even if you felt pretty frail to begin with.

If the garden is calling to you, it may do good to more than just your spirits. Clare Cooper Marcus, professor emeritus at the University of California in Berkeley, has found that being out in nature lowers blood pressure, relieves muscle tension, and lowers stress.

Gardening without a garden

If you have no garden and don't have access to an allotment, does that mean you can't garden at all? Actually, indoor gardening is a hobby too: there's likely to be less exercise in it, but window-ledges, indoor planters, wall-hung herb gardens, mounted pallets (you just get a standard builder's pallet and plant in the gaps), and even bonsai can be a lot more rewarding than you'd expect. Indoor gardening is increasingly popular in these days of small flats, so look online or talk to someone at your local garden centre: there are plenty of solutions to the problem of space. Anything green is good, so be inventive and make a happy space for yourself.

? HOW DOES YOUR GARDEN GROW?

There are as many different gardens as there are gardeners, but if you're planning a new project you may find that creating a particular type of garden – one that expresses what's most important to you – will give you the greatest pleasure over the years. Consider these options:

1 **The kitchen garden**. Few things are nicer than eating your own home-grown fruit and veg (apart from serving them up to your family, of course).

2 **The wildlife garden**. Nature is under pressure, especially so in urban environments, so if you avoid using weedkiller and leave some undergrowth, your local creatures may be thankful. Dig a pond, and frogs may pay a visit to eat your garden pests, or plant buddleia for a butterfly paradise.

3 **The contemplative zone**. If what you really want is a peaceful spot to sit in, try going minimalist. Bamboo is easy to grow. Keeping it in check may be a problem, so choose a non-invasive species. The bamboo will provide a beautiful screen from the everyday world.

4 **The easy-access garden**. If your joints are not what they used to be, too much bending may cause you more pain than pleasure. The solution is raised beds: how high you raise them is up to you, but even as little as 45cm (18in) can ease the strain of bending down to work on them.

5 **The sensory garden**. If your eyesight is on the wane, does that mean there's no joy in nature for you? Far from it: this is the time to plant with a focus on other senses. We all love scented flowers, of course, but don't overlook sound features such as a trickling fountain, or texture, by choosing thornless flowers with soft, strokeable leaves. Even blind people can enjoy a well-designed garden, so think creatively.

NEW KID ON THE BLOCK
THE RETIRED ENTREPRENEUR

Governments call small businesses "the engine-room of the economy". If you've still got work energy to spare, do you fancy keeping those engines turning during retirement by starting a business of your own?

We all know the image of the energetic young entrepreneur, but studies suggest that actually older people are likely to be better at founding and running a business than their younger counterparts. Not everyone's a natural manager, of course, but if you feel you've got it in you, then retirement might be the time.

The safe pension
One of the biggest reasons people hesitate to become self-employed, as a 2009 study by the not-for-profit-organization the RAND Corporation points out, is the fear of losing their pension: if you're working for a company that offers you a safety net for your old age, it's an unusual (and perhaps a rash) individual who gambles that. On the other hand, a 2015 Canadian study reported that older workers are most likely to start their own business after a period out of the labour market: they begin when they get access to their public pension funds. It's never wise to invest more of your pension than you can afford to lose, of course, but knowing it's secure can open a door to trying a life as your own boss.

The hobby business
Do you have a skill you'd like to turn into cash? Some retired entrepreneurs simply use their work skills, but suppose you have a talent that looks like it might make you money – what then? The most successful working hobbyists tend to be those who start small and work up: a market stall or online shop can be a great place to test the waters without putting too much pressure on your finances or your sanity. But remember: your former leisure activity may no longer be the restful activity it once was when it starts having deadlines and bottom lines associated with it – so you may need a new hobby!

The retired inventor
A lifetime of experience can give you insight into what people need, and therein lies the path to invention. More than 60 per cent of the United Inventors Association are over 50, and it's not just men tinkering in their sheds: as their president Warren Tuttle points out, women can be extremely creative because they see the benefit of a product and then work backwards. As US psychiatrist Dr Gary Small points out, "An aging brain can see patterns better." Again, the advice

DOES SOCIETY DISCOURAGE THE OLDER ENTREPRENEUR?

Most of us do better with some encouragement, and the idea of starting a business in a world that thinks you're too old is hardly heartening. Does that mean social attitudes put older people off starting businesses? According to a 2009 US study, it's somewhat more complicated than that: we filter society's expectations through our personal experiences and attitudes.

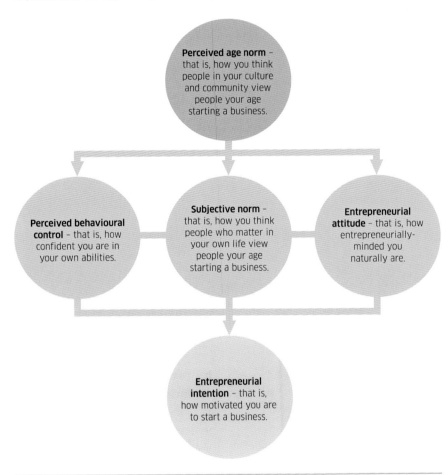

Perceived age norm – that is, how you think people in your culture and community view people your age starting a business.

Perceived behavioural control – that is, how confident you are in your own abilities.

Subjective norm – that is, how you think people who matter in your own life view people your age starting a business.

Entrepreneurial attitude – that is, how entrepreneurially-minded you naturally are.

Entrepreneurial intention – that is, how motivated you are to start a business.

is to start small – applying for a patent, for example, can actually end up costing more than it's worth because the technical requirements are high. Some people do use intermediary companies that take a (rather large) cut of the profits in exchange for handling licensing. If you can keep the costs manageable, however, the creativity of coming up with new things can benefit your brain as well as your finances. Being an entrepreneur isn't easy, but if you like a life of excitement, isn't that part of the appeal?

Q WHAT MAKES AN ENTREPRENEUR?

Social psychologist David McClelland proposed, in 1961, that entrepreneurs show three psychological traits:

■ They prefer a challenge.

■ They accept personal responsibility for outcomes.

■ They are innovative.

Sixten years later, social psychologist Albert Bandura, added a set of qualities for the "self-efficacy" (ie belief in oneself) an entrepreneur needs:

■ Prior experience.

■ Having role models (see pp90–91) in one's own life.

■ Being supported or persuaded by other people.

Other psychologists in the 1980s and 90s pointed out that it's not all personal: the economy needs to be in a state that will favour enterprise, and some groups of people, such as men and people with more education, tend to have an advantage. More recently, psychologists have added that sheer practicality, such as access to funds, business networks, and resources are always critical.

It seems that a lot of factors make an entrepreneur – do you see your own profile here?

YOU ARE NEVER TOO OLD TO SET ANOTHER GOAL OR TO DREAM A NEW DREAM

C. S. LEWIS
AUTHOR AND POET

THE SOUL AT EASE

SPIRITUALITY AND CALM

Would you call yourself a religious person? How about a spiritual or a philosophical one? With work no longer eating up time, retirees often find their thoughts turning more to the eternal.

If your faith speaks of an afterlife, your feelings about retirement are probably somewhat different from the feelings of someone who doesn't believe in Heaven or reincarnation. Studies generally suggest that people who believe in a loving deity tend to be less stressed by age and illness – but as far as practical advice goes, that has its limits: you can't become religious just for the good of your psychological health. Can psychology give us guidance about achieving inner peace that applies equally well to the religious and the non-religious?

Religion versus spirituality

Would you equate religion with the realm of the spirit? There can be an overlap, but psychologists tend to view the two as somewhat distinct: when they speak of "religion", they mean belief in a creed, whereas "spirituality" means a state of being based on an awareness of transcendence. The latter doesn't necessarily have to be based on religious beliefs – some of the most passionate atheists argue that wonder at the physical universe is a form of transcendence in itself, and a 2009 study for the *Journal of Psychology* found that a faith in "nature and humanity" had a similarly positive effect on people's wellbeing. If you hold anything sacred, then psychologically speaking that's a powerful resource.

Mindfulness and meditation

If you are religious, you almost certainly know how to pray, but whether you are or not, do you know how to meditate? Scientists have prescribed meditation as part of the treatment for anxiety, stress, and pain management, and the results suggest it does make a difference.

That said, meditation teachers argue that meditating just for the physical benefits is somewhat missing the point: to really enjoy meditation, we have to approach it as an end in itself.

So, how do you meditate? The central principle is this: you gently bring your awareness right into the present moment. You can do it anywhere – walking, gardening, doing the dishes – but here is a simple form of meditation to do sitting down:

- **Sit somewhere comfortable** (but not so comfortable that you'll fall asleep) and relax.
- **Be aware of the sensations** you're feeling in your body – your feet, your back, the balance of your head – but don't try to change anything.
- **Quietly focus** on your breathing: experience the rise and fall of your chest, the sensation in your lungs. Try counting exhalations (up to ten then starting over), then inhalations: this relaxes you, then energizes you.
- **Thoughts will enter** your mind. Don't worry about them; just let them pass without either pursuing them or trying to force them out. Likewise, you'll hear sounds around you. Just let them wash over you. Mindfulness is compatible with almost any belief system, and the studies suggest that practising mindfulness and meditation techniques truly does you good. Try to build time into your day for a short meditation – it might improve your mental, and even your physical health.

Q THE MINDFUL BRAIN

Does mindfulness really help? According to brain scans, absolutely: research has found actual physical differences in the brains of regular meditators:

- It shrinks the amygdala, the "fight or flight" part of the brain associated with anxiety.

- It reduces activity between the anterior cingulate cortex, which registers painful sensations as unpleasant, and the prefrontal cortex, which processes our thoughts and feelings. Regular meditators, exposed to painful stimuli, show more brain activity in the "pain centres", but report feeling less pain.

- It thickens the prefrontal cortex, associated with higher-order functions such as concentration, thought, and problem-solving.

- It results in a similar pattern of brain waves to the ordinary brain at rest.

According to a study at Beth Israel Deaconess Medical Center in 2013, meditation might actually slow the progress of Alzheimer's, too.

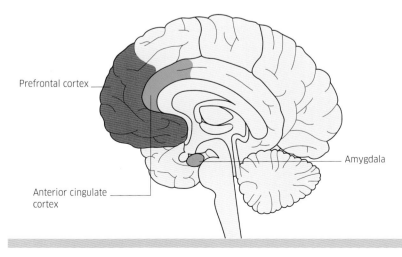

Prefrontal cortex

Anterior cingulate cortex

Amygdala

MAKING IT HAPPEN

TIME MANAGEMENT IN RETIREMENT

Now you're in charge of your own schedule, how's your time management? Do you organize your time so that you get everything done that you want, or do the days just seem to slip away from you?

Work may be stressful, but there's one thing you can say for it: having deadlines imposed from outside and colleagues you don't want to let down can keep even the least motivated among us fairly productive. Post-retirement, productivity may not be your top priority, but as you'll have a happier life if you engage in at least some activities such as exercise and personal projects, you'll still have things you want to get done. However, with no one to account to except yourself (and possibly friends and family, but they can't exactly fire you), how do you get the most out of the time you have and how do you save yourself from procrastination?

Time speeding up?

When we're children, a day seems to last a year, but older adults often feel as if time is racing past. That's hardly how

> Planning is **bringing the future** into the present so that you can **do something** about it now.
>
> **Alan Lakein**
> Author and time
> management expert

you want to feel in retirement: most of us would like to get the maximum benefit out of the time we have.

What's going on here? Well, according to US neuroscientist David Eagleman, time is a "rubbery thing", and our perceptions of time are stretched and compressed by how much information we need to process. In childhood, more or less everything is a new experience, and therefore a new lesson for the brain. Once we reach retirement age, on the other hand, we tend to know most of what we need to know to get by. The brain doesn't need to learn as much – and hence, we start experiencing fast time.

Ready for a challenge?

If you want to feel like time lasts in retirement, then, the solution is to challenge your brain. Intense emotions can do it – a 2011 experiment by neuropsychologist Sylvie Droit-Volet, for example, found that people watching scary films experienced subjectively slower time than people who watched sad or neutral ones. However, if you don't want to spend your time alarming yourself, the solution is probably to find new things to learn. You can read more about adult education on pp198–99, but the message seems to be that if you want to experience a schoolboy's or schoolgirl's sense of endless

THE ART OF FEELING GOOD

When there are things to do, we need a bit of energy to get them done – but at the same time, getting them done can energize us. What psychologists refer to as "subjective wellbeing" (ie, how good you think you feel) can operate in a virtuous circle with progress on our tasks. Get even a bit done, and your subjective wellbeing goes up – which in turn, keeps you progressing.

SUBJECTIVE WELLBEING   **PROGRESS**

days, your best bet is to do what they do and find yourself some kind of course.

Putting things off

In the early days of retirement, not having to do anything can feel like a luxury – but as time goes on, it can turn into a burden. The ironic thing is, studies suggest, that far from being laid-back idlers, serious

procrastinators tend to suffer from more stress than people who just get on with things – and when it comes to putting off things like medical appointments, procrastination can be positively dangerous. We know we feel better if we get things done, so why do we delay?

A lot of it has to do with what psychologists call "emotional regulation" – that is, the ability

>> to manage our feelings. A 2003 study by Canadian psychologist Fuschia Sirois, for example, found that procrastination was related to feeling less competent; we're all less motivated to do things we fear we might fail at, and a low opinion of our own efficacy tends to weaken any good intentions.

Short-term thinking

Another study by Sirois in 2010 found that procrastinators were more likely to rationalize: if they'd made a problem worse by addressing it too late, their tendency was to say "Well, at least I caught it when I did" rather than "I wish I'd caught it sooner" – meaning that there was less motivation to change their habits. The overall problem is fairly simple: procrastinators have difficulty doing an effective cost-benefit analysis of how they spend their time, and hence have an above-average tendency to choose a short-term relief (or avoid a short-term inconvenience) at the cost of facing a bigger problem later.

We all want to make the best use of our time in retirement. Getting ourselves organized can be harder for some of us than for others, but with careful time management, we might just be able to achieve what we've always wanted: long days to do what we truly want.

Q AN EFFICIENT MIND

Getting things done is part of what scientists refer to as "executive function", which means the ability to organize the information we possess, make good decisions based on it and act on those decisions. If our own executive function isn't great, does that mean we're doomed to a lifetime of putting things off?

Not necessarily: what it does mean is that we benefit from more systematic planning. Ideas for improving our executive function include:

1 **Take regular** aerobic exercise. This will keep the brain stimulated.

2 **Break tasks** down into lots of small sub-tasks. This reduces the sense of feeling overwhelmed.

3 **Make an agreement** to complete tasks by a set time. In retirement, you might benefit from bringing in a spouse or friend as a kind of "coach" who can check in on you and make sure you're staying on top of things. You might even impose consequences for missing the deadline – nothing too bad (you're supposed to be enjoying retirement, after all), but try

betting a small sum or agreeing that you'll do something fun if you make it.

4 **Try to limit** how many things you do at once. Switching between tasks is an executive function skill; if you're working on building it up, start small.

5 **Cut down** on the distractions. Procrastinators tend to go for small short-term pleasures, so limit your access to them until you've got something done.

6 **Use routines**. Everyone benefits from these to some extent, but if your executive function isn't the strongest, they will be particularly helpful.

You don't have to do all of these things – if you don't feel very able to organize yourself, a long list can be overwhelming in itself – but try to do some and see what works best.

THE PROCRASTINATING BRAIN

How does our executive function (see left) work? It happens in the brain's prefrontal cortex, and is measured on the following nine scales:

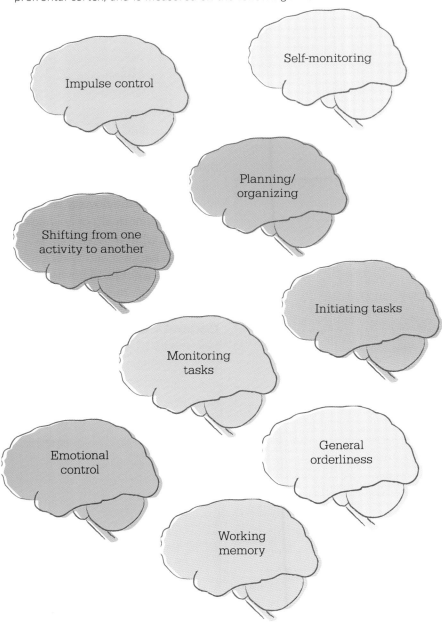

Impulse control

Self-monitoring

Planning/organizing

Shifting from one activity to another

Initiating tasks

Monitoring tasks

Emotional control

General orderliness

Working memory

According to a 2011 study by US psychologist Laura Rabin, people who procrastinated tended to have problems with all nine scales – in other words, the procrastination was part of a general difficulty with organizing.

Q ENOUGH HOURS IN THE DAY?

If you're a busy retiree, you may just feel there's not enough time to get everything done. Actually, a 2014 study published in the *Journal of Marketing Research* found that people were prone to overestimating the amount of time they needed for various tasks. Of course, sometimes we do have to cut things out of our schedule, but the researchers also pointed out that anxiety can be a positive emotion if you reframe it: try saying to yourself "I'm excited" and see if the worry starts to feel more like motivation.

80%

SETTING THE PACE

A 2007 Brazilian study tested a group of subjects with an average age of 63 who had to **undergo a boring experience** – in this case, sitting still for four hours of dialysis. Over 80 per cent of them reported feeling **time went faster when they listened to music** than if they sat in silence. In fact, those listening to a waltz were slightly more likely to report this effect than those listening to a march – but unlike with the march, the waltz also had a few volunteers who found time going slower. If you have to endure a dull medical experience, perhaps a two-four tempo is more reliable.

HOW'S IT GOING?

REGULAR SELF-ASSESSMENTS

Sometimes it's easy to get into a rut. Suppose you have a routine established, but you're not exactly happy and you're not sure why: what can you do to get some clarity?

Once we settle into retirement, we may need to keep an eye on our emotional wellbeing. According to a 2012 study in the *Journal of Happiness Studies* by the psychologist Elizabeth Mokyr Horner, people tend to experience a "sugar rush" in retirement: the immediate aftermath is full of pleasure and excitement, but once the "rush" has passed, their mood crashes.

There may be many reasons for this, but once the novelty wears off the "new normal", only we can recognize what it takes to make ourselves happy – and we may need to give our self-knowledge a bit of a boost to do a good job.

Understanding who you are
Sometimes working life is so busy we don't really have time to question what sort of person we actually are. If you've mastered the Internet, however (see pp148–51),

Q STANDING TALL

Our posture can actually affect our mood: numerous studies have found that if we sit up straight or take up a powerful pose that makes us feel confident, we're more likely to think positively. So check your body language and try to keep it upbeat. On a more concrete level, it's also a smart plan to measure your height regularly, especially if you're a woman: it's a good way to catch early any problems with decreasing bone density.

the good news is that there are plenty of ways to assess yourself. The term you need to search for is "psychometric test". These are often used by employers to determine who's right for which job, but in fact they're not job-specific, they're based on psychology proper. Two particularly popular ones are:

- **The Five Factor Test**. This measures what psychologists call the "Big Five", often referred to by the acronym "OCEAN":
  1) **O**penness (to new experiences).
  2) **C**onscientiousness.
  3) **E**xtraversion/introversion.
  4) **A**greeableness.
  5) **N**euroticism.
- **The Myers-Brigg** Type Indicator. Based on the theories of Carl Jung and his successors, it measures four different aspects of the psyche:
  1) Introversion vs extraversion.
  2) Intuition vs sensing (whether you're concrete and rational or abstract and intuitive).
  3) Thinking vs feeling (whether you make decisions with your head or your heart).
  4) Judging vs perceiving (whether you're more comfortable with having matters settled or keeping decisions open).

There are no "right" or "wrong" answers; taking one of these tests may just give you more perspective on how you think and feel.

❓ WHAT QUESTIONS SHOULD YOU ASK YOURSELF?

Try giving yourself an "interview" to see what it reveals about your ambitions. Questions to ask yourself are:

- **What and who** do I love most in the world? (Be sure to ask yourself "what" and "who" as two separate questions: we all need relationships, but think about who you are as an individual, too.)
- **If I had a magic wallet** that always produced more money, how would I live?
- **If I was going to live forever**, what would I do?
- **If I knew I was going to die** in a month's time, what would I do?
- **If someone asked me**, "How do you know you're a good person?", what would I want to be able to say?
- **If I were fearless**, what would I do?
- **If I were a great artist** and created a self-portrait, what – other than an image of myself – would I include? (For example, what background or objects?)

Humans have an evolutionary tendency to be a bit negative: spotting bad things is more likely to keep us alive than spotting good things. By cultivating self-knowledge, however, we can get a better sense of what would feel satisfying for us as individuals in the long term.

PERF-ECT HEALTH
If you're feeling low, it could be that you're a bit run-down physically. Regular medical checks are a good idea, and in between, remember this useful acronym:

P **P**roduce – eat fresh fruit and vegetables.

E **E**xercise – stay as active as you can.

R **R**elaxation – try to have at least 15 minutes of laughter and enjoyment every day.

F **F**ibre – keep your digestive system healthy.

GOING FOR GOLD

HOW TO LIVE THE FUTURE

What's the soundest way to "live the good life" once we're no longer working? We may have individual goals for retirement, but what we all want, in the end, is to be happy.

You've earned the right to feel good once you settle into retirement. Life may throw some curve balls, but we all want to achieve a state of mind where we feel satisfied and rewarded even if things aren't perfect. What, psychologically speaking, is the answer?

Living your values

When we live in retirement, the chances are that we think a lot about what really matters to us. How do we choose what to care about the most? US social psychologist Shalom Schwartz identifies four basic sets of values:

- **Self-enhancement** – achievement, being admired.
- **Self-transcendence** – thinking beyond yourself, concern for the welfare of others and the world (see opposite).
- **Openness to change** – flexibility, imagination, pleasure, and independence.
- **Conservation** – upholding traditions, maintaining security of individuals and society.

Self-enhancement is important for younger adults, but studies suggest that retirees worry about it less. Having a positive relationship with the other three is what makes us happiest as we age. There's no reason to give up on achievement and admiration entirely – but once our working life is done, thinking in bigger terms is often the best path towards that goal.

Positive psychology

An influential movement in the field is "positive psychology" – studying what makes us happy. We do best when we can live well with ourselves, other people, and the world around us. The Pursuit of Happiness, Inc defined seven habits of happy people:

- **Relationships** – we don't need many, but we need the ones we have to be supportive places where we can express ourselves.
- **Caring** – kindness to others tends to make us happier.
- **Exercise** – keeping physically active is good for our mentality.
- **Flow** – a joyful state where we're engaged with a challenge and everything seems to come together.
- **Spiritual engagement** and meaning – not necessarily formal religion (see pp208–09), but reaching for something beyond ourselves.
- **Strengths and virtues** – finding and using our talents and good qualities.
- **A positive mindset** – a sense of optimism, mindfulness, and gratitude.

A wide range of studies have confirmed that these habits are good for everyone, including retirees. What's really important is still there for us and always will be.

How, then, should we be happy in retirement? It's as unique as ourselves, and as universal as our humanity.

Q THE POWER OF REMINISCENCE

Do you have to live only for the future? Psychology suggests that memory empowers all of us – and two kinds of remembering are particularly helpful for older people. Canadian psychologists Paul Wong and Lisa Watt identify them thus:

Instrumental reminiscence
Memories that give us a sense of competence and continuity – for example, remembering a time when you were able to overcome or resolve a problem.

Integrative reminiscence
Memories that give us a sense of self-worth, coherence, and reconciliation with the past – for instance, remembering insights and positive relationships.

We can always look forward and hope for good things to come, but by the time you retire you'll have a treasure-house of memories. Pick out the best ones for contemplation, and you'll be well on your way to mastering what psychologists call "successful aging".

SELF-TRANSCENDENCE

Psychologist Shalom Schwartz talks about "self-transcendence": how do we go about it? His theories suggest three ways to reach beyond ourselves:

Seeking...	What we reach for	Virtues
Ultimate meaning	Reaching beyond our physical limitations towards something bigger than our own understanding.	Faith, idealism, goodness, truth, and beauty.
Situational meaning	Reaching beyond the limits of our circumstances to connect with our deepest values.	Mindfulness, openness, curiosity, and compassion.
Your calling	Reaching towards the greater good, employing your interests and talents.	Generosity, responsibility, and connectedness to humanity.

INDEX